HONOR'S REWARD

HOW TO ATTRACT GOD'S FAVOR AND BLESSING

Devotional Workbook

JOHN BEVERE

COVER, INTERIOR DESIGN & PRINT PRODUCTION:
Eastco Multi Media Solutions, Inc.
3646 California Rd.
Orchard Park, NY 14127
www.eastcomultimedia.com

Written and edited by: Vincent M. Newfield • www.preparethewaytoday.org

Design Manager: Aaron La Porta
Designers: Heather Wierowski, Aaron La Porta

Printed in Canada

TABLE OF CONTENTS

QUICK OVERVIEW & SUGGESTIONS FOR USE

Welcome to the *Honor's Reward Devotional Workbook*. We are privileged to present to you this in-depth companion study to John Bevere's inspiring book. Much prayer and research have been poured into the book you now hold. We believe it is not by accident that you are doing this study, and we expect God to do great things in your life through it.

In order to help you get the *maximum* benefit from this material, please read through this brief overview and these suggestions for use. The workbook and devotional contains 12 chapters that correspond to the 12 DVD video sessions. Each chapter is based on one or more chapters in the book and contains a series of related questions, activities, a devotional, and an area to journal your learning experience and spiritual journey.

EACH CHAPTER CONTAINS...

- Truths to Treasure – related promises and principles from God's Word. We encourage you to meditate on the message of each of these Scriptures and commit them to memory. Nothing on earth has the power to change your life like the Word of God!

- Lessons from Leaders – a powerful assortment of quotes from outstanding Christian leaders of the past and present. These words from the wise help emphasize and add understanding to the depth of the topic being discussed. So take a moment or two to "chew" on what they have to say.

- Instant Replays – wisdom worth remembering from John's teaching. It has often been said that repetition is the best teacher. So, to help drive home the powerful points John makes throughout the teaching, we offer these creative capsules that recapture the best of the best.

- Dig Deeper – creative activities designed to give you an even richer understanding of honoring others. This "hands-on" section will help you to practically apply each teaching right where you live.

- Honor Principles – a condensed summary of the main thrust of each chapter. Hiding these significant "sound bites" of wisdom in your heart will help you retain the essence of the message presented.

You will also discover many eye-opening definitions, fascinating facts and heartfelt prayers to help deepen your relationship with the Father. At the end of each chapter, we have provided space for you to *Express Your Experience*—a place for you to journal your thoughts, feelings and anything the Holy Spirit reveals or speaks to you. These entries are priceless and well worth taking the time to write.

WE SUGGEST YOU...

- *Read the corresponding chapters* in John's book, *Honor's Reward*, watch the DVD video session and then complete the chapter in the workbook and devotional.

- *Begin and end each of your study sessions with prayer.* Invite the Holy Spirit to teach you and guide you into all truth (see John 16:13). If you ask, He will give you insight and understanding to all you are studying, and as you finish each session, ask Him to permanently seal the truths you have learned in your spirit and soul.

- *Pace yourself* to complete each chapter of the workbook and devotional during the week. You may want to make it a part of your daily routine or set aside two or three nights a week to work through the questions and activities. Realize, this is your *personal* study with the Lord, and there is no right or wrong way to do it.

- *Be consistent in your study.* Whatever time and place you decide to do the workbook and devotional, stick to it. If you fall behind, don't quit. Push through it, even if it takes you longer than you planned. You will reap a great reward for the time and energy you invest.

- *Be honest with yourself and God as you answer each question.* Knowing the truth of God's Word along with the truth about yourself will bring freedom to your life that can be found no other way.

We can't emphasize enough the importance of prayer and welcoming the Holy Spirit to teach you. James 4:5 says He yearns to be welcomed into every part of your life. Our prayer for you is that God "...may grant you a spirit of wisdom and revelation [of insight into mysteries and secrets] in the [deep and intimate] knowledge of Him, by having the eyes of your heart flooded with light, so that you can know and understand the hope to which He has called you, and how rich is His glorious inheritance in the saints..." (Ephesians 1:17,18 AMP).

Please Note: Unless otherwise noted, Scripture passages in the video sessions and the workbook are taken from the New King James Version (NKJV). Some New Living Translations (NLT) are taken from the Second Edition.

"We are all making a crown for Jesus out of these daily lives of ours, either a crown of golden, divine love, studded with gems of sacrifice and adoration, or a thorny crown, filled with the cruel briars of unbelief, or selfishness, and sin..."

—Aimee Semple McPherson[1]

1 HONOR

Please refer to Chapters 1 and 2 in the *Honor's Reward* book along with Session 1 of the teaching series.

HONOR

The esteem due or paid to worth; high estimation; a testimony of esteem; any expression of respect or of high estimation by words or actions.

–American Dictionary of the English Language, **Noah Webster 1828**

---

1. Many modern movies display heroic scenes of great courage and sacrifice. Recall one of the most memorable scenes from a favorite film in which someone was honored for their bravery and sacrifice. Why did it move you?

    _____

    _____

    _____

    _____

    _____

    _____

    _____

2. Why do you think this type of honorable courage is virtually extinct in society today? What negative character traits seem to abound and discourage people from giving sacrificially and being courageous?

    Check Out 2 Timothy 3:1-5, taking a close look at verse 2

    _____

    _____

    _____

    _____

    _____

LESSONS from LEADERS

"Courage is not limited to the battlefield or the Indianapolis 500 or bravely catching a thief in your house. The real tests of courage are much quieter. They are the inner tests, like remaining faithful when nobody's looking, like enduring pain when the room is empty, like standing alone when you're misunderstood."

—*Charles Swindoll*[2]

3. John describes a person who has faithfully lived out their life calling for Christ as someone with a *Grandfather* or *Grandmother Anointing*—when they speak the wise listen. Who in your life would you say walks in a *Grandfather* or *Grandmother Anointing*? How have they made a positive impact on your life, and how can you show them honor?

_____

_____

_____

_____

4. What are three common qualities of a seasoned saint of faith who has walked well and walked long the paths of life?

a. _____

_____

b. _____

_____

c. _____

_____

Check Out Hebrews 10:36 for wisdom worth remembering

5. Why is it so important to persevere, endure and finish strong?

_____

_____

_____

_____

_____

INSTANT Replay

"Christianity is not a sprint but an endurance run.
Therefore it is not how we *start* the race that counts, but how we
complete it. How we *finish* is determined by the choices we make,
and those are often formed by patterns we develop along the way."

—John Bevere (Page 3)

6.   In 1 Kings 12, we find the story of Rehoboam rejecting the wisdom of his father's counselors and how it cost him dearly. Looking back on your own life, what wise counsel did you *reject* and what did it cost you? What wise counsel did you *receive*, and how were you blessed?

_____

_____

_____

_____

_____

7.   For Rehoboam, his decision to reject the wisdom of his father's counselors was a *life-defining moment*. Describe in your own words what a life-defining moment is. List two or three life-defining moments you have experienced, and tell how they are still affecting you.

_____

_____

_____

_____

_____

_____

_____

_____

> *Truths to Treasure*
>
> "Look to yourselves, that we do not lose those things we worked for, but that we may receive a *full* reward."
>
> —*2 John 8 NKJV*

8.   In what way did God describe Himself to Abram? Is this aspect of His character the same for us today?

Check Out
Genesis 15:1
Check Out
Hebrews 11:6

_____

_____

_____

_____

_____

9.   What is the significance and implication of the phrase "that we may receive a *full* reward" in 2 John 8, and what does that mean to you?

_____

_____

_____

_____

_____

10. *Complaining* is one of the greatest ways we can lose our reward and miss out on God's will for our lives. It can easily become a *negative pattern* of dishonor if we are not careful. *Thankfulness*, on the other hand, is a *positive pattern* of honor that paves the way to God's best.

   a. List some positive patterns of behavior in your life that you want to see increase.

   _____

   _____

   _____

   _____

   b. List some negative patterns of behavior in your life that you want to see change.

   _____

   _____

   _____

   _____

LESSONS from LEADERS

"*Rewards* should never be used as a payoff to a child for not disobeying. That becomes a bribe—a substitute for authority. For example, Mom is having trouble controlling her three-year-old in a supermarket. 'Come here, Pamela,' she says, but the youngster screams, 'No!' and runs the other way. Then in exasperation Mom offers Pam a sucker if she'll come quickly. Rather than rewarding obedience, Mom has actually reinforced the child's defiance."

–*Dr. James Dobson* [3]

11. Far too many believers attempt to build their Christian lives without the elementary teaching of _____.
As a result, they are missing a major part of the _____ _____ of their faith.

Truths to Treasure

"For we must all appear before the judgment seat of Christ, that each one may receive the things done in the body, according to what he has done, whether good or bad."
–*2 Corinthians 5:10 NKJV*

12. The words "eternal judgment" in Hebrews 6:1,2 mean there will never be:
    a. A sin that God will not forgive
    b. Any alterations, amendments or changes made to those judgments
    c. An opportunity to be forgiven for the wrong we've done
    d. A reason to believe that we can lose the rewards we have earned on earth

13. Read 2 Corinthians 5:9-10. In what ways do these verses challenge you?

    Check Out
    Ephesians 2:8,9
    Check Out
    1 Corinthians 3:13-15

    _____

    _____

    _____

    _____

    _____

INSTANT *Replay*

"What we do with the cross determines *where* we'll
spend eternity; however, the way we live as believers
determines *how* we'll spend it."
—John Bevere (Page 8)

14. Developing godly *patterns* in our lifestyle not only carries the promise of reward at the judgment seat of Christ but also blessings in this life as well (see 1 Timothy 4:8). In what practical ways have you experienced blessings for godly choices that you have made?

    _____

    _____

    _____

    _____

    _____

15. What powerful promise of reward does Jesus give us that is worth remembering?

    Check Out
    Mark 10:29,30

    _____

    _____

    _____

    _____

LESSONS *from* LEADERS

"There is an essential difference between the decease of the godly and the death of the ungodly. Death comes to the ungodly man as a penal infliction, but to the righteous as a summons to his Father's palace. To the sinner it is an execution, to the saint an undressing from his sins and infirmities. Death to the wicked is the king of terrors. Death to the saint is the end of terrors, the commencement of glory."

–Charles H. Spurgeon [4]

John gives a simplistic literal definition of the Greek word *time*, which we translate as *honor*. He defines it as "a valuing, something weighty or precious, appreciation, esteem, favorable regard and respect." Take a moment to list some practical ways you can begin to express honor to your...

Parents _____

_____

_____

_____

_____

Take To Heart: Exodus 20:12; Matthew 15:4; Ephesians 6:2

Spouse _____

_____

_____

_____

_____

Take To Heart: 1 Peter 3:1-9; Ephesians 5:22-33;
Colossians 3:18,19,23-25

Pastor/Christian Leaders _____

_____

_____

_____

_____

Take To Heart: Galatians 6:6; 1 Thessalonians 5:12,13;
1 Timothy 5:17

GREAT EXPECTATIONS

"Now, He *could do no* mighty work there, except that He laid His hands on a few sick people and healed them."
—Mark 6:5 NKJV

HONOR PRINCIPLE 1
Honor or dishonor can be displayed in deed, word or thought. But all true honor originates from the heart.

In chapter two, John addresses in detail how Jesus was received when He returned to His home-town of Nazareth. Mark 6:5 declares that Jesus was *unable* to do mighty miracles in their midst—not be-cause He didn't want to but because something was restraining Him. What suppressed the Savior? The answer is found in Mark 6:4: They were *offended* by Jesus, and their offense caused them to withhold honor from Him. The people of Nazareth did not see Him as *extraordinary*, only *ordinary*. They were familiar with Jesus, and to them, He was just a common local—there was nothing special about Him.

When Jesus read from the book of Isaiah and then proclaimed He was the Messiah, the people were greatly offended. They had a mental image of how the Messiah would come and what He would be like, and their minds were *closed* to anything that did not fit their im-age. They had "great expectations" of a conquering king who would come and rescue them from Roman oppression. But their expecta-tions were incomplete—they had not accurately interpreted the Scrip-tures. As a result, they dishonored Jesus and missed their time of a divine visitation from God.

INSTANT Replay

"...Often God will send us what we need in a package we don't want.
Why? To let us know He's God and we cannot second-guess Him.
We cannot search for answers with merely our heads....
Scripture cannot be interpreted from our limited, human,
mental understanding. There must be a breath of the Spirit of God.
He alone gives wise counsel and correct application."
—John Bevere (Page 14)

Expectations are great and we should have them. We just need to give God the freedom to manifest His power as He chooses. By ex-pecting God to do great things in and through our lives when we seek Him or gather in His name,[5] we are honoring Him—we are valuing His presence as precious and priceless. Expecting God to move in our lives is an expression of our faith.

The question is, what are you **expecting**? When you join with others each week to worship the Lord, learn His ways and serve in ministry, do you *expect* Him to show up and show out? How about in your everyday life? Consider this insightful passage from A. W. Tozer written nearly a half century ago:

"True faith is never found alone; it is always accompanied by expectation. The man who believes the promises of God *expects* to see them fulfilled. Where there is no *expectation* there is no faith.

> ...One characteristic that marks the average church today is lack of anticipation. Christians when they meet do not *expect* anything unusual to happen; consequently only the usual happens, and that usual is as predictable as the setting of the sun.

> ...Christian expectation in the average church follows the *program*, not the *promises*. Prevailing spiritual conditions however low, are accepted as inevitable. What will be is what has been. The weary slaves of the dull routine find it impossible to hope for anything better.

> We need today a fresh spirit of anticipation that springs out of the promises of God. We must declare war on the mood of nonexpectation, and come together with childlike faith. Only then can we know again the beauty and wonder of the Lord's presence among us."

—A.W. Tozer[6]

MEDITATE ON THE MESSAGE

Reread Tozer's observations. Can you identify with what he is saying? In what ways do his remarks apply to your church and to you personally?

_____
_____
_____
_____
_____
_____
_____
_____
_____

Are you open to allowing God to move in the way He chooses?

_____

_____

_____

_____

In what areas of your life has your mind-set remained rigid about how the Lord should move in your life?

_____

_____

_____

_____

_____

_____

Ponder the Promise

"The intelligent man is always open to new ideas. In fact, he looks for them."

—*Proverbs 18:15 TLB*

Prayer

Father, I come to You through the finished work of Jesus Christ. I ask You to forgive me for "boxing" You in. I'm sorry for having such a rigid mind-set at times of how You should or shouldn't be worshipped, who You should and shouldn't bless, and how You should or shouldn't do something. I set You free to work in whatever way You want—in my life and in the lives of others (include specific names of people the Lord brings to mind). Help me to **expect** *you to move and manifest Your goodness in my life each and every day in whatever ways You want, through whomever You want. In Jesus' name, Amen.*

EXPRESS YOUR EXPERIENCE

Take a few moments to reflect upon this week's session on honor and *express your experience* in writing. What are some of the most important principles the Holy Spirit is showing you? What Scripture really struck a chord with you? Is there anything else that the Holy Spirit is speaking to your heart?

_____

_____

_____

_____

_____

_____

CHEW ON THIS...

Meditate on this personalized Scripture and say it out loud each day for the next week. Write down what the Lord shows you and any changes He makes in you.

"And therefore the Lord [earnestly] waits [expecting, looking, and longing] to be gracious to *[me]*; and therefore He lifts Himself up, that He may have mercy on *[me]* and show loving-kindness to *[me]*. For the Lord is a God of justice. Blessed (happy, fortunate, to be envied) are all those who [earnestly] wait for Him, who **expect** and look and long for Him [for His victory, His favor, His love, His peace, His joy, and His matchless, unbroken companionship]!"

–Isaiah 30:18 AMP

_____
_____
_____
_____
_____
_____
_____
_____
_____
_____
_____
_____
_____
_____
_____
_____
_____
_____
_____
_____
_____
_____

(1) *What Shall I Do with Jesus*, Pt II, This Is That, 1923 (www.creativequotes.com, retrieved 5/21/07). (2) Quotes on Courage, Charles Swindoll (www.leadershipnow.com, retrieved 5/21/07). (3) James Dobson, *Solid Answers* (Tyndale House Publishing: Wheaton, IL, 1997) p.127. (4) www.spurgeon-gems.org (retrieved 5/19/07). (5) See Matthew 18:20. (6) A. W. Tozer, *A Treasury of A. W. Tozer, A Collection of Tozer Favorites* (Christian Publications, Inc.: Harrisburg, PA, 1981) pp.257-259.

Notes

"Aim at heaven
and you will get
earth thrown in.
Aim at earth and
you get neither."

–*C.S. Lewis*[1]

2 YOUR FULL REWARD

Please refer to Chapter 3 in the *Honor's Reward* book along with Session 2 of the teaching series.

FULL REWARD

Second John 8 says, "Look to yourselves, that we do not lose those things we worked for, but that we may receive a *full* reward" (NKJV). The word **full** means "abundant, complete, entire, supplied, saturated, containing the whole of the matter."

—*American Dictionary of the English Language,* **Noah Webster 1828**

1. In Luke 7 and Matthew 8, we find the detailed account of the Roman centurion who came to Jesus to receive healing for his paralyzed servant. This was a person who was "outside" the family of God—he was not an Israelite. In light of his response, Jesus said He had not found anyone with such great faith in Israel. What *two* things made the centurion's faith so great and enabled him to receive his *full* reward?

    _____

    _____

    _____

    _____

    _____

    _____

    _____

    _____

    _____

    _____

    _____

FASCINATING FACT:
A Roman legion consisted of 6000 soldiers with one commander over the entire legion. There were 60 centurions who reported to the commander, and each centurion had 100 soldiers under him.

2.   We will each receive rewards for the things we do for Christ—in heaven *and* here on earth. We will be rewarded fully, partially or not at all. Using the people from Scripture we have studied so far, separate into categories those who received a full, partial or no reward and give the reason(s) why.

FULL _____

_____

_____

_____

_____

PARTIAL _____

_____

_____

_____

_____

NO REWARD _____

_____

_____

_____

_____

Check Out
Luke 17:5-10

3.   Here we see a direct relationship between mountain-moving faith, submission to authority and honor. What important attitude toward authority displayed in verse 10 is an essential ingredient for our faith to be effective?

_____

_____

_____

_____

_____

LESSONS from LEADERS

"The will of God for your life is simply that you *submit yourself* to Him each day and say, 'Father, Your will for today is mine. Your pleasure for today is mine. Your work for today is mine. I trust You to be God. You lead me today and I will follow.'"

–*Kay Arthur* [2]

_____

_____

_____

_____

_____

_____

_____

4. Another person who received a full reward is the Syro-Phoenician woman who sought Jesus to deliver her daughter from a demon that was tormenting her. The Bible says that after multiple requests, Jesus finally answered her saying, "Let the children be filled first, for it is not good to take the children's bread and throw it to the little dogs" (Mark 7:27 NKJV).

a. How do you think *you* would react to this response from Jesus?

_____

_____

_____

_____

b. What major trap of the enemy did the Syro-Phoenician woman avoid falling into?

_____

_____

c. What does the woman's response tell you about her perspective of Jesus? What aspect of Jesus' character was she appealing to?

Read
Mark 7:28

_____

_____

_____

_____

5. In the midst of desperate situations, both the Roman centurion and the Syro-Phoenician woman recognized Jesus' authority and chose to honor Him. Looking back on your own life, can you recall a time when you chose to recognize God's authority over your circumstances and honor Him *instead* of complaining or getting upset? Describe it.

_____

_____

_____

_____

_____

_____

_____

_____

_____

INSTANT *Replay*

"Honor is an *essential key* to receiving from heaven....
Those who honor God will be honored. That is just the way
it works. Everyone who honored Jesus received from
God in the proportion the honor was rendered."

—John Bevere (Page 25)

6. In Mark 14 we find the story of Jesus and the woman with the alabaster jar of perfume. It was costly and worth about one year's wages. While Jesus was reclining at the table, she broke the jar and poured the perfume over His head, symbolically anointing Him for burial.

    a. Verses 4 and 5 tell us that some were angry and criticized her, saying the perfume should have been sold and the money given to the poor. Jesus saw her act as honorable *worship*. Have you ever criticized someone for the way in which they worshiped God? How does reading this account help you see situations like this in a new light?

    _____

    _____

    _____

    _____

Check Out
2 Samuel
6:14-23

    b. It tells how Michal, King David's wife, despised David's dance of celebration before the Lord—his act of worship. What happened to her as a result? What do you think her condition symbolizes, and what can we learn from it?

    _____

    _____

    _____

    _____

LESSONS *from* LEADERS

"You must not look on the esteem of your fellowmen as being the reward of excellence, because often you will meet with the *reverse*: you will find your best actions misconstrued and your motives misinterpreted."

—Charles Spurgeon[3]

7. Jesus told those around Him that they would always have the poor with them, but *He* would not always be with them. The woman with the alabaster jar recognized the *window of opportunity* to honor Jesus in a significant way, and she seized it.

   a. We can't honor Jesus *directly*, but we can honor Him by seizing the opportunities He gives us to honor others. **Write out** and **take to heart** the related power principle in Matthew 25:40,45.

   _____
   _____
   _____
   _____

   b. How is the woman with the alabaster jar of perfume still being honored today? (Check out Mark 14:9.)

   _____
   _____
   _____
   _____

8. Taking John 13:20 and John 5:23 together in context, we discover that two words are interchangeable, or synonymous. What are they?

   _____
   _____
   _____
   _____
   _____

> *Truths to Treasure*
>
> "Most assuredly, I say to you, he who receives whomever I send receives Me; and he who receives Me receives Him who sent Me."
> —*John 13:20 NKJV*

9. Those who honored Jesus were actually honoring the Father. Yet, in John 5:41, Jesus said, "I do not receive honor from men." We know from Scripture that people honored Jesus, so what did He do with the honor given to Him?

   _____
   _____
   _____
   _____
   _____
   _____
   _____
   _____
   _____

10. Jesus Christ was *fully God*, yet on earth He was flesh and blood like us and ministered as the *Son of Man*. Why do you think He told the people He healed not to tell anyone? What was He guarding himself from? What can we learn from this?

_____

_____

_____

_____

_____

_____

_____

_____

_____

_____

LESSONS from LEADERS

"In Jesus we will see how both as the *Son of God* in heaven, and as *man on earth*, He took the place of entire subordination. He gave God the honor and the glory which is due Him. And what He taught so often was made true to Himself: 'He that humbleth himself shall be exalted' (Luke 18:14)."

–Andrew Murray[4]

INSTANT Replay

"The word *dishonor* means to treat as common, to treat as ordinary. When you speak of dishonor to a Greek man, he thinks of something that can be easily dealt with or done away with— something light that has no substance, such as vapor."
—John Bevere (Teaching Session 2)

11. In 1 Samuel 2:30 NIV God says, "...Those who honor me I will honor, but those who despise me will be *disdained.*" The word disdain means...
    a. To remove the spot or soiled area from something (or someone)
    b. A disagreement between two people
    c. To permanently cut off and do away with forever
    d. The feeling that someone is unworthy of consideration or respect

12. How does God consider those who dishonor Him? Do you think this has any effect on their prayers being answered?

_____

_____

_____

_____

_____

13. In your own words, explain the connection between *offense* and *dishonor*?

_____

_____

_____

_____

_____

In this week's session, we learned that while on earth, Jesus was heaven's connection to the Father. Therefore, a tangible way to honor the Father was by treating His Son with honor. For us today, a tangible way to honor Jesus is by honoring those He has called and sent to represent Him, especially pastors, teachers, evangelists and missionaries. Read Galatians 6:10 below and ask the Lord to show you some specific things you can do to honor the Christian leaders in your life this week and in the weeks and months ahead.

> *Truths to Treasure*
>
> "When pride comes, then comes *dishonor*, but with the humble is wisdom."
>
> *—Proverbs 11:2 NASB*

IDEA STARTERS

- Send an email of encouragement, emphasizing your appreciation for one of their godly qualities.
- "Snail" mail a card of thanks for their faithful investment in your life.
- Make a brief phone call and express your appreciation for something specific they have done (leave a voice message if necessary).
- Give them a gift certificate to their favorite restaurant, coffee shop or bookstore.

> *Truths to Treasure*
>
> "So then, as occasion and *opportunity* open up to us, let us do good [morally] to all people.... Be **mindful** to be a blessing, especially to those of the household of faith [those who belong to God's family with you, the believers]."
>
> *—Galatians 6:10 AMP*

My plan to bless my [pastor, evangelist, missionary, spiritual parent] includes...

_____

_____

_____

_____

_____

_____

_____

_____

Hide in Your Heart

HONOR PRINCIPLE 2
"...Those who honor me I will honor, but those who despise me will be disdained."
–1 Samuel 2:30 NIV

_____

_____

_____

_____

_____

_____

_____

_____

_____

THE CHAIN OF COMMAND

"Let every person be loyally subject to the governing (civil) authorities. For there is no authority except from God [by His permission, His sanction], and those that exist do so by God's appointment."

—Romans 13:1 AMP

There is a definite common thread that runs throughout session two—the theme of authority. Understanding the structure of spiritual authority, and then honoring those at each level, is essential to receiving honor's reward. John clearly explains that there is an authority structure in the Kingdom of God. It begins with God the Father and flows to Jesus, the One He sent and gave all authority to (see Matthew 28:18). In the same way, Jesus gives us authority and sends us out to continue the work He began (see Matthew 10:1; Mark 6:7; Luke 9:1,2; 10:19).

Each of us makes up a different part of the Body of Christ (see 1 Corinthians 12:12-31), and we are each given authority to function in our role. There are some who are over us, some who are under us, and some on the same level with us. God has established this structure of authority to bring health and protection to His body. He has promised that if we will faithfully stay where He has planted us, in due time He will exalt us (see 1 Peter 5:6).

MEDITATE ON THE MESSAGE

There is no one born on the face of the earth who does not have a God-ordained chain of command over them—not even Jesus. **Read** Luke 2:41-52 for an eye-opening examination of truth.

Describe the "umbrella of protection" Jesus came under in this situation. How did He respond to them? How was He blessed?

Check Out
verse 51
verse 52

_____

_____

_____

_____

_____

_____

According to verse 49, Jesus had a burning passion to fulfill His destiny, yet something wasn't right. What was it? Has a situation like this ever happened to you? Describe it.

_____

_____

_____

_____

_____

_____

What are the three levels of spiritual authority under God recognized by Jesus in Matthew 10:40-42? What does each one mean?

P_____: _____

_____

_____

_____

R_____: _____

_____

_____

_____

L_____: _____

_____

_____

Ponder the Promise

"He who receives you receives Me, and he who receives Me receives Him who sent Me. He who receives a prophet in the name of a prophet shall receive a prophet's reward. And he who receives a righteous man in the name of a righteous man shall receive a righteous man's reward. And whoever gives one of these little ones only a cup of cold water in the name of a disciple, assuredly, I say to you, he shall by no means lose his reward."
—Matthew 10:40-42 NKJV

Check Out
Ephesians
4:11

In the New Testament, the first level of authority is divided into five segments. List them in the space provided.

(1) _____   (4) _____

(2) _____   (5) _____

(3) _____

Given the three levels of authority from the question above, write the names of the people in authority *in your life* whom you interact with the most, placing them in the appropriate category.

P_____   R_____   L_____

_____   _____   _____

_____   _____   _____

_____   _____   _____

_____   _____   _____

To which of these people are we to show honor? Are we rewarded for just showing honor to those above us?

_____

_____

_____

_____

_____

_____

INSTANT *Replay*

"The only way to have true authority is to be under authority."
—John Bevere (Teaching Session 2)

Prayer

Father, I humbly ask You to forgive me for rebelling against the authorities You have placed over me. To rebel against them is to rebel against You, and I don't want to do that anymore. Please help me obey and submit to my pastor, my employer and everyone else You have placed over me. Give me the grace, Your supernatural strength and ability, to submit to those in authority who are difficult, immature and abrasive. Help me pray for them, not talk about them. With You, I can do all things. Thank You for Your mercy, and thank You for rewarding my life as I honor those You have placed over me. In Jesus' name, Amen.

EXPRESS YOUR EXPERIENCE

Take some time to reflect upon what it means to receive a *full* reward and then *express your experience* in writing. What part of this session really hit home with you? Is the Holy Spirit pointing out anyone in authority specifically that you've had problems with? What specific action is He asking you to take?

_____

_____

_____

_____

_____

_____

_____

_____

_____

_____

_____

_____

_____

_____

_____

_____

_____

_____

_____

_____

_____

_____

_____

_____

_____

_____

_____

_____

_____

_____

_____

(1) Quotes by C.S. *Lewis* (www.brainyquote.com, retrieved 6/7/07). (2) Christian quotes on submitting your life to God (www.dailychristianquote.com, retrieved 6/26/07). (3) Charles Spurgeon, *The Second Coming of Christ* (Whitaker House: New Kensington, PA, 1996) pp. 35,36. (4) Andrew Murray, *Humility* (Whitaker House: New Kensington, PA, 1982) pp. 21,22.

"If I *belittle* those whom I am called to serve, talk of their weak points in contrast perhaps with what I think of as my strong points; if I adopt a superior attitude, forgetting 'Who made *thee* to differ [disagree with, be at odds with] and what hast thou that thou hast not received?' then I know nothing of Calvary love."

–*Amy Carmichael*[1]

CHAPTER 3

HONORING AUTHORITY

Please refer to Chapters 4, 5 and 6 in the *Honor's Reward* book along with Session 3 of the teaching series.

AUTHORITY

Legal power or a right to command or to act; as the authority of a prince over subjects and of parents over children; government; the persons or the body exercising power or command; as the local authorities of the states.

—American Dictionary of the English Language, **Noah Webster 1828**

INSTANT *Replay*

"Before continuing to discuss a prophet's or leader's reward,
we must first cover the importance or value of *authority*.
Once this truth is established in our heart, we can *sincerely*
and more *effectively* honor those over us."
—John Bevere (Teaching from Session 3)

1. Name the four divisions of divine delegated authority spoken of in the New Testament and give everyday examples of each.

C_____ – _____

_____

S_____ – _____

_____

F_____ – _____

_____

C_____ – _____

_____

2. **Write out** and **take to heart** God's instructions regarding authority in the following Scriptures. Identify which division of authority each verse exemplifies. (See pages 43, 44 in chapter 5 for help.)

ROMANS 13:6,7 (TEV)

_____

_____

_____

_____ Example of: _____

1 TIMOTHY 6:1 (ASV)

_____

_____

_____

_____ Example of: _____

EPHESIANS 6:2,3 (NKJV)

_____

_____

_____

_____ Example of: _____

1 THESSALONIANS 5:12,13 (NLT)

_____

_____

_____

_____ Example of: _____

3. **Write out** the definitions of _democracy_ and _kingdom_.

a. **DEMOCRACY** _____

_____

_____

_____

_____

_____

_____

This is what the Kingdom of God is _not_.

> ### Truths to Treasure
>
> "_Obey_ your leaders, and _submit_ to them; for they keep watch over your souls, as those who will give an account. Let them do this with joy and not with grief, for this would be _unprofitable for you._"
> —_Hebrews 13:17 NASB_

b. **KINGDOM** _____

_____

_____

Search the Scripture: Luke 17:20,21; John 18:36; Romans 14:17; 1 Corinthians 4:20; James 2:5.

c. Which definition best describes *your* understanding of God's divine structure of authority? In what way does this challenge your current mindset?

_____

_____

_____

_____

d. How do you think seeing God's kingdom with a democratic point of view makes it difficult to understand the things of God? Why do you think this has caused division in the church?

_____

_____

_____

FASCINATING FACT:
Many Americans believe America was founded as a democracy, but this was not the case. The original intent and accomplishment of America's Founding Fathers was to establish a *constitutional republic*, not a democracy. By definition, a true *democracy* is a government in which the will of the majority rules—whatever the majority *thinks* and *feels* is right is what becomes law. A *constitutional republic*, in contrast, is a government in which sovereign power resides in the hands of representatives who are elected by the people and pass laws that uphold the Constitution. The source of the Constitution and laws that govern America is unquestionably the Bible. Noah Webster declared: "Our citizens should early understand that the genuine source of correct republican principles is the Bible...."[2]

INSTANT *Replay*

"The English word *appointed* in [Romans 13:1] is the Greek
word *tasso*, which means, 'to assign, ordain, or set.'
In no way does this word have 'by chance' implications.
It is direct appointment."
—**John Bevere** (Page 46)

4. According to Romans 13:1,2, where does all legitimate authority come from? For what purposes is authority established?

    _____

    _____

    _____

5. When we oppose or rebel against people in authority, we are actually opposing and rebelling against who?
    _____. (See page 46.)

6. To *oppose* means "to resist, be against, contradict or fight." We have all opposed people in authority at some point in our lives, and one of the most dangerous ways is with our words. Proverbs 18:21 declares "Death and life are in the power of the tongue... (NKJV)."

    Check Out the story of Moses and the Israelites in Exodus 16:1-12, 17:1-7 and Numbers 20:1-6

    a. How do our words become a weapon in the hands of the enemy against those in authority?

        _____

        _____

        _____

        _____

    b. Who in authority in your life have you opposed, resisted and been against? How did you oppose them? If you could turn back time, what would you do differently?

        _____

        _____

        _____

        _____

    c. **Write out** the related power principle found in Philippians 2:14.

        _____

        _____

        _____

        _____

        _____

        _____

        _____

Truths to Treasure

"...I exhort first of all that supplications, prayers, intercessions, and giving of thanks be made for...all who are in authority, that we may lead a quiet and peaceable life in *all* godliness and *reverence*. For this is good and acceptable in the sight of God our Savior."

–1 Timothy 2:1-3 NKJV

7.   In light of 1 Timothy 2:1-3, God wants us to use our mouth to...

      a.   expose the errors and ungodliness of all those in authority
           every chance we get.
      b.   pray for and not talk or complain about the people He has
           placed in authority over us.
      c.   pray for our church leaders only and keep quiet about
           government officials.
      d.   point out the problems of those in authority and pray God
           brings judgment upon them.

8.   God's Word clearly states that *all authority* is established *by
      God*, but it does not say all authority is *godly*. There are a number
      of ungodly leaders mentioned in Scripture that God raised up,
      including Pharaoh (Exodus 9:16; Romans 9:17), King Saul (1
      Samuel 15:10,11), and King Nebuchadnezzar (Jeremiah 43:10).
      These authority figures were often violent and hostile to God's
      ways and His people, persecuting individuals for doing right.

      a.   How does it make you feel when you are persecuted, or
           treated badly, by someone in authority for doing what is
           right? What emotions rise up in you?

           _____

           _____

           _____

      b.   Suffering for doing good is something very few Christians
           care to discuss, yet it is a part of our lives as believers.   **Read**
           What do these verses say to *you* about suffering?   Philippians
                                                                            1:29,30;
           _____   2 Timothy 2:3
                                                                           and 1 Peter
           _____   2:20,21

           _____

LESSONS from LEADERS

"The breaking of the alabaster box and the anointing of the Lord filled the house
with the odour, with the sweetest odour. Everyone could smell it. Whenever you
meet someone who has really *suffered*; been limited, gone through things for the
Lord, willing to be imprisoned by the Lord, just being satisfied with Him and nothing else, immediately you scent the fragrance. There is a savour of the Lord. Something has been crushed, something has been broken, and there is a resulting odour
of *sweetness*."

                                                                    —Watchman Nee[3]

9. Thankfully, God has promised to *never* leave us or forsake us (see Deuteronomy 31:6; Matthew 28:20; Hebrews 13:5). Through Jesus Christ we have open access to the Father who will gladly give us the supernatural strength we need to make it through tough times. **Write out** and **take to heart** the powerful promises found in these scriptures:

a. Isaiah 40:29 _____
   _____
   _____
   _____

b. 2 Corinthians 12:9 _____
   _____
   _____
   _____

c. Hebrews 4:15,16 _____
   _____
   _____
   _____

d. James 4:6 _____
   _____
   _____
   _____

For an eye-opening exploration of truth, **check out** these verses in *The Amplified Bible.*

e. 1 Peter 5:5b _____
   _____
   _____
   _____

10. There is *one* condition or time in which we are *not* to obey someone in authority. What is it, and what must we still be very careful to do? Give an example from Scripture and include an example from your own life.

   _____
   _____
   _____
   _____
   _____
   _____
   _____

INSTANT Replay

"To say we honor authority, yet refrain from submission and obedience to it, is to deceive ourselves. To *honor* authority is to *submit* to authority; we dishonor authority by not submitting to it."
—John Bevere (Page 41)

11. Explain the important difference between *submission* and *obedience* with regards to our attitude and our actions.

_____

_____

_____

_____

_____

> **Check out** Isaiah 1:19 and Hebrews 13:17 for wisdom worth remembering.

12. Here's a question we've all heard and probably even asked: Does God want us to submit to harsh, ungodly people in authority who mistreat us? As hard as it may be to swallow, the answer is *yes*. First Peter 2:18 confirms this. Why does God want us to submit to cruel, crooked and unjust leaders? The answer can be summed up in three words: *for our benefit.*

List the three biblical benefits of submitting to, or honoring, harsh leaders.

a. The **FIRST** reason to submit/honor harsh, ungodly authority is (see 1 Peter 2:20-23):

_____

_____

_____

b. The **SECOND** reason to submit/honor harsh, ungodly authority is (see 1 Peter 3:9):

_____

_____

_____

c. The **THIRD** reason to submit/honor harsh, ungodly authority is (see Romans 5:3,4; Hebrews 5:8,9; James 1:2-4):

_____

_____

_____

LESSONS from LEADERS

"I have discovered that in almost every case, God wants us to be submissive to those He has placed over us—even if we don't agree with them or they are in error. The only time God does *not* want us to submit to authority is when we are asked to do something that either goes against our conscience or causes us to sin. In other words, you and I should be submissive to our boss, our governing officials, our pastor and everybody else that is in authority over us unless it puts us in disagreement with God's Word."

—Joyce Meyer[4]

13. In chapter six of the book, John shares a story of a man who was purposely overlooked for a promotion he was rightfully due. Instead of taking matters into his own hands, he chose to submit to the unjust authority over him and leave the matter in God's hands. By honoring those in authority who mistreated him, God set him up to receive a *full* reward.

    a. Has a situation like the one described ever happened to you? Explain how you handled it. Did you miss out on being promoted or did you receive a full reward?

    _____

    _____

    _____

    _____

    _____

    b. As we choose to *stay put* where God places us and not run from difficulty, we will be rewarded. We may face "fiery trials," like Shadrach, Meshach and Abed-Nego, but if we honor the authority over us, we will be promoted. **Write out** and **take to heart** the powerful promises found in 1 Peter 5:6,10.

    _____

    _____

    _____

    _____

    _____

    _____

    _____

    _____

    _____

Truths to Treasure

"For not from the east nor from the west nor from the south come promotion and lifting up. But God is the Judge! He puts down one and lifts up another."

—Psalm 75:6,7 AMP

John shares a few stories from ministers he is acquainted with who have experienced mighty miracles as they have traveled around the world preaching the Gospel. Blind eyes and deaf ears have been opened, the lame have been made to walk, tumors have been destroyed, and incurable diseases have been obliterated.

These *same* ministers with the *same* message, *same* anointing and *same* ministry technique have returned to America and other western nations and have witnessed only a *few* manifestations of God's healing power. Why? It all has to do with *honor*. Honor opens the door to the miraculous—withholding honor and giving dishonor close it. When these ministers of God are treated with honor—value, high esteem, appreciation—the power of God flows like a river, saturating and satisfying thirsty souls.

John also points out that what happens in a service has very little to do with who's teaching and a lot to do with the congregation's *reception*. When the minister is received with *reverence* and *respect* as one sent by God, great things take place. But when he is viewed as just another person filling the pulpit, extraordinary moves of the Spirit are missing.

Think for a moment... How do you treat your pastor, associate pastors and Sunday school teachers? Do you honor them with your actions, words and thoughts? Or do you lightly esteem them?

_____

_____

_____

_____

_____

_____

When was the last time you received deep revelation of truth from your pastor/teachers? What was it? Do you get something out of the messages on a regular basis?

_____

_____

_____

_____

_____

Remember, the way we receive our spiritual leaders *directly* affects how we receive insight from the Lord.

Scripture clearly shows that Eli was a poor example of both a parent and priest (see 1 Samuel 2). Yet, Hannah responded to his insensitive insult with respect and humility. Have you ever experienced a situation with a spiritual leader like this? Describe it and tell how you responded.

_____

_____

_____

_____

_____

_____

_____

_____

_____

_____

_____

_____

_____

_____

Romans 12:21 states that we overcome evil with good. In other words, when someone in authority is insensitive or insulting, don't insult them or spread gossip about them. Instead, look for ways to be good to them. Take some time to brainstorm with

> ### Truths to Treasure
> "Do not be overcome by evil, but **overcome evil with good**."
> –*Romans 12:21 NIV*

the Holy Spirit some specific things you can do to be a blessing to the spiritual leader(s) in your life who have been harsh with you. Remember, when you honor those who dishonor you, God will see to it that you are blessed!

I PLAN TO BLESS _____ BY:

1. _____
2. _____
3. _____
4. _____
5. _____
6. _____
7. _____

FREEDOM THROUGH FORGIVENESS

"For if you forgive people their trespasses [their reckless and willful sins, leaving them, letting them go, and giving up resentment], your heavenly Father will also forgive you. But if you do not forgive others their trespasses [their reckless and willful sins, leaving them, letting them go, and giving up resentment], neither will your Father forgive you your trespasses."

—Matthew 6:14,15 AMP

From the moment you and I are born to the day we leave this earth, we will be under someone's authority. And at times the authority we are under will be harsh and even ungodly, creating ample opportunity to be offended by their actions. This means we need to learn how to release and forgive them.

It is clear from Scripture that God is the author, or establisher, of all authority—even those who are cruel. However, He is not the author of man's cruelty; man is responsible for his own cruel actions, not God. By His grace, we can learn how to submit to those who are over us. It is important to realize that the ability to submit to authority in the *present* is based on having freedom and forgiveness toward the authorities who hurt us in the *past*. It is also an outflow of the fear of the Lord.

INSTANT Replay

"The fear of the Lord in a person's heart says to its leader, 'I'm aware of the authority on you, that it originates from God. Therefore, you already have my respect and honor. You don't have to earn it.'"
—John Bevere (Page 57)

Get alone with God and take some time to allow Him to search your heart. Ask Him to show you what frustrates, irritates and aggravates you the most about harsh, unjust leaders.

_____

_____

_____

_____

_____

Is the Holy Spirit showing you any specific situation(s) in your past when you experienced unfair or abusive treatment from someone in authority? Describe it (knowing no one else will see your answers).

_____

_____

_____

_____

_____

_____

_____

_____

_____

_____

_____

_____

_____

_____

_____

_____

_____

_____

_____

It is normal to feel hurt, angry and even enraged toward the people in authority who have mistreated you. But know that God does not want you to stay that way. He wants to heal the wounds within your soul with the soothing, penetrating power of His love. All He asks is for you to want to release and forgive the person who hurt you. He will then take your hand and walk you through the process of forgiveness, bringing you to the point where you are able to pray and bless the person who hurt you.

Prayer of Forgiveness and Freedom

Father, I am hurting deeply because of the way _____ [person's name – could be a teacher, coach, parent, grandparent, church worker, employer, etc.] treated me. Their words/actions were wrong, but I know that I cannot hold on to this hurt. According to what Jesus said in Matthew 6:14,15, I need to release _____ [person's name] and forgive them. The truth is, I don't feel like doing it, but I want to want to do it. So, as an act of my will, I choose to release and forgive _____ for _____ [what they did].

Forgive me for holding on to unforgiveness toward them. Wash me clean with the precious blood of Jesus (see 1 John 1:9). Create in me a clean heart, renew a right spirit in me and restore unto me the joy of my salvation (see Psalm 51:10-12).

By the power of Your grace, I choose to bless _____ [person's name]. I ask you to bless them physically, mentally, emotionally, spiritually and relationally. Give them wisdom beyond their years, health in their body, and an on-fire relationship with you. [In any way you would want to be blessed, pray for them to be blessed.]

Thank you for healing me, Father, from the inside out. And thank you for giving me the strength to pray for and not talk about _____ [person's name] every time I begin to feel the pain of what they did. In Jesus' name, Amen!

Beloved, realize that you *cannot* heal the hurts within you—otherwise you would have done so already. God is the *only* One Who can heal your hurts and give you renewed hope and peace. Yes, we are to work out our salvation with reverence and the fear of the Lord, but as Philippians 2:13 declares, "[Not in your own strength] for it is **God** Who is all the while effectually at work in you [energizing and creating in you the power and desire], both to will and to work for His good pleasure and satisfaction and delight" (AMP).

REMEMBER: FORGIVENESS IS A PROCESS

Don't mistake the delay in *feeling* like you have forgiven someone as evidence that you haven't forgiven them. Just as a deep gash from a kitchen knife takes more time to heal than a paper cut, the deeper the hurt, the more time it takes to *fully* heal. Read this insightful story, and see if you can relate:

Corrie ten Boom, a survivor of a WWII Nazi concentration camp, told of not be-

Ponder the Promises

"And I am convinced and sure of this very thing, that **He** Who began a good work in you will continue until the day of Jesus Christ [right up to the time of His return], developing [that good work] and perfecting and bringing it to full completion in you."
—*Philippians 1:6 AMP*

"Now may the God of peace make you holy in every way, and may your whole spirit and soul and body be kept blameless until our Lord Jesus Christ comes again. **God will make this happen**, for he who calls you is faithful."
—*1 Thessalonians 5:23,24 NLT*

"May **God**, who puts all things together, makes all things whole...put you together, provide you with everything you need to please him...."
—*Hebrews 13:20,21 The Message*

ing able to forget a wrong that had been done to her. She had forgiven the person, but she kept rehashing the incident, and as a result, was unable to sleep. Finally, Corrie cried out to God for help in putting the problem to rest.

"His help came in the form of a kindly Lutheran pastor," Corrie wrote, "to whom I confessed my failure after two sleepless weeks."

'Up in the church tower,' he said, nodding out the window, 'is a bell which is rung by pulling on a rope. But you know what? After the sexton lets go of the rope, the bell keeps on swinging. First ding, then dong. Slower and slower until there's a final dong and it stops. I believe the same thing is true of *forgiveness*. When we forgive, we take our hand off the rope. But if we've been tugging at our grievances for a long time, we mustn't be surprised if the old angry thoughts keep coming for a while. They're just the 'ding-dongs' of the old bell slowing down.'

"And so it proved to be. There were a few more midnight reverberations, a couple of dings when the subject came up in my conversations, but the force—which was my willingness in the matter —had gone out of them. They came less and less often and at the last stopped altogether: we can trust God not only above our emotions, but also above our thoughts."[5]

If someone in authority hurt you and you have forgiven them but can't seem to totally escape the thoughts and feelings of what they did, don't buy the lie of the enemy that you haven't forgiven them. Give it to God and give Him some time. As you surrender your will to His, He will change your feelings and make them come into agreement with your will to forgive.

LESSONS from LEADERS

"I *surrendered* unto Him all there was of me; everything! Then for the first time I realized what it meant to have *real* power."

–*Kathryn Kuhlman*[6]

EXPRESS YOUR EXPERIENCE

As we close this week's session, get quiet once again before the Lord. More than likely, He is doing a deep healing work in your soul at this moment. Don't rush through what He is doing. As Psalm 46:10 says, "Be still and know that [He] is God... (NIV)." Let Him show you anything and everything He desires and write down any insights He reveals, as well as any necessary actions He asks you to take.

(1) Quotes by Amy Carmichael (www.dailychristianquote.com, retrieved 7/16/07). (2) David Barton, *Original Intent: The Courts, the Constitution, and Religion* (Aledo, TX: Wallbuilders, 1996) pp. 335-337. (3) Quotes by Watchman Nee (www.dailychristianquote.com, retrieved 7/16/07). (4) *A Balanced Look at Submission to Authority*, Joyce Meyer, Life In The Word magazine, June 2001, Joyce Meyer Ministries, Inc., Fenton, MO). (5) Illustrations on forgiveness (www.sermonillustrations.com, retrieved 7/17/07). (6) Quotes by Kathryn Kuhlman (www.dailychristianquote.com, retrieved 7/17/07).

"The care of human life
and happiness, and not
their destruction, is the first
and only legitimate object
of *good government.*"

–*Thomas Jefferson*[1]

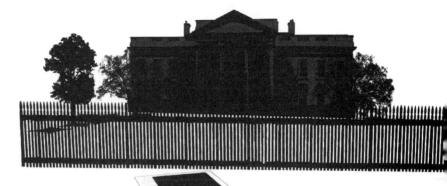

4 HONORING CIVIL LEADERS

Please refer to Chapter 7 in the *Honor's Reward* book along with Session 4 of the teaching series.

CIVIL

Relating to the community or to the policy and government of the citizens and subjects of a state; as in the phrases, civil rights, civil government, civil privileges....

—American Dictionary of the English Language, **Noah Webster 1828**

---

1. People serving as civil leaders are the *natural gatekeepers* of our towns, cities, states and nations. **Write out the definition of the word gatekeeper.**
Gatekeeper _____
_____
_____
_____
_____
_____

2. What feelings well up inside you when you see a policeman, fireman, judge, senator, governor, etc.?
_____
_____
_____
_____
_____
_____

Truths to Treasure

"Would you like to be unafraid of those in authority? Then do what is good, and they will praise you, because they are *God's servants* working for your own good. ...They are *God's servants* and carry out God's punishment on those who do evil. For this reason you must obey the authorities—not just because of God's punishment, but also as a matter of conscience. That is also why you pay taxes, because *the authorities are working for God* when they fulfill their duties. Pay then what you owe them; pay them your personal and property taxes, and *show respect and honor for them all.*"

—Romans 13:3-7 TEV

3. Knowing that our attitudes about everything are shaped, to a great degree, during our childhood, what was the attitude of your parents toward civil leaders?

    _____

    _____

    _____

    _____

    _____

4. Generally speaking, what is the attitude of most people, including many Christians, toward civil leaders? This includes policeman, politicians and other public servants.

    _____

    _____

    _____

    _____

    _____

INSTANT *Replay*

"What good does it do when we are *criticizing* our leaders
in our homes, small groups, and church services and supporting
those who do the same? That is nothing more than *backbiting*.
What we say in private we must be willing to say with a heart
burning with love and honor before the face of our leaders.
If not, we will poison our spirits and it will manifest
in the presence of our leaders."
—John Bevere (Page 78)

5. Name the group of people in the New Testament who were notorious for being judgmental, critical faultfinders.

    _____

    _____

    _____

> *Truths to Treasure*
>
> "...For it is written, 'You shall not speak evil of a ruler of your people.'"
> *—Acts 23:5 NKJV*

Check out
Revelation
12:9,10

6. Another name for a faultfinder is an *accuser*. Who in Scripture is known as the "accuser of the brethren"? _____
    So when we judge, criticize, find fault with and accuse others, who are we acting like? _____.

7. Judgment is reserved for God and God alone. **Write out** and **take to heart** the related power passage found in Romans 12:18-21.

_____

_____

_____

_____

_____

8. Having a *judgmental* and *critical* spirit toward people in civil authority is dangerous and opens the door for the enemy to bring problems into our lives. **Write out** and **take to heart** these words of warning:

    a. Matthew 7:1,2

    _____

    _____

    _____

    _____

    _____

    b. Luke 6:36-38

    _____

    _____

    _____

    _____

    _____

    c. James 4:11,12

    _____

    _____

    _____

    _____

    _____

LESSONS from LEADERS

"Never *believe* anything bad about anybody unless you positively know it to be true; never tell even that unless you feel that it is absolutely necessary—and that God is listening while you tell it."

—*William Penn*[2]

9. The NASB version of Proverbs 6:16-19 describes *sowing discord* as "one who spreads strife." The Message Bible conveys it as "a troublemaker," and the NIV calls it "stirring up dissension." Although some news organizations and ministries mean well in reporting the news, they tend to be a major source of discord among people, including Christians.

> ### Truths to Treasure
>
> "There are six things the LORD *hates*—no, seven things he detests: haughty eyes, a lying tongue, hands that kill the innocent, a heart that plots evil, feet that race to do wrong, a false witness who pours out lies, **a person who sows discord** among brothers."
>
> —*Proverbs 6:16-19 NLT*

a. Describe the way *you* feel after watching, listening to or reading the news.

_____

b. The opposite of discord, strife and dissension is *peace* and *unity*. **Read** and **meditate on the message** of Psalm 133. What powerful benefits does God give to those whose aim is to live in peace?

_____

_____

_____

LESSONS from LEADERS

"When you throw dirt at people you're not doing a thing but losing ground."

—*Zig Ziglar*[3]

10. A *bad reputation* with people *outside* the church...
   a. is not very important nor is it something we should be concerned with.
   b. has little or no effect on the spreading of the Gospel.
   c. has little or no effect on the people of the community.
   d. hinders the Gospel from being preached and diminishes a Christian's ability to speak to the community.

> ### Truths to Treasure
>
> "Furthermore, *[church leaders]* must have a good reputation and be well thought of by those outside [the church], lest *[they]* become involved in slander and incur reproach and fall into the devil's trap."
>
> —*1 Timothy 3:7 AMP*

11. Philippians 2:7 KJV says that Jesus "...made himself *of no reputation*, and took upon him the form of a servant, and was made in the likeness of men." What does this mean and how does it *not* conflict with 1 Timothy 3:7?

_____

_____

_____

_____

_____

_____

_____

12. How were early believers at the church in Jerusalem viewed by people *outside* the church?

Check out
Acts 5:13

_____

_____

_____

_____

_____

_____

_____

13. **Write out** and **take to heart** the related power principle found in Proverbs 22:1.

_____

_____

_____

_____

_____

_____

_____

LESSONS from LEADERS

"My brethren, let me say, *be like Christ at all times. Imitate him in 'public.'* Most of us live in some sort of public capacity—many of us are called to work before our fellow-men every day. We are watched; our words are caught; our lives are examined—taken to pieces. The eagle-eyed, argus-eyed world observes everything we do, and sharp critics are upon us. Let us live the life of Christ in public. Let us take care that we exhibit our Master, and not ourselves—so that we can say, 'It is no longer I that live, but Christ that lives in me.'"

—*Charles Spurgeon*[4]

INSTANT Replay

"Jesus said, 'He who [honors] a prophet in the name of a prophet shall receive a prophet's reward.' He specifically spoke of church authority, but recall that the spiritual laws of authority often span the borders to *all areas* of authority. So it could also be said, 'He who honors *civil authority* in the name of *civil authority* shall receive the reward civil authorities carry.' What is their reward? The answer is **the key to the community**."
—John Bevere (Page 71)

14. So far, we have learned that one of the ways God wants us to honor our civil leaders is by not speaking evil of them. Another way you and I are to honor our authorities is to *pray for them*. What are some specific biblical ways you can pray for your civil leaders—especially those who are harsh and ungodly? **Check out** and **write out** the prayer principles from the following Scriptures:

a. **Ephesians 1:17,18** (taking into account Acts 9:17,18 and 2 Corinthians 4:4)

_____
_____
_____
_____
_____

b. **1 Timothy 2:4** (also taking into account verses 1-3)

_____
_____
_____
_____

c. Is there any other prayer principle from Scripture that comes to mind?

_____
_____
_____
_____
_____

15. When Peter was arrested and thrown into prison, believers in the early church fervently prayed for God's help. They kept their mouths free of criticism and their hearts full of the fear of the Lord. What are the three specific results of their prayers mentioned in the following Scriptures?

a. Acts 12:5-19 _____

_____

_____

_____

_____

b. Acts 12:20-23 _____

_____

_____

_____

_____

c. Acts 12:24 _____

_____

_____

_____

_____

INFO TO GO

Join the "Concert of Prayer" for our God-appointed civil leaders!
Here is a helpful list of ministries and organizations that are rallying people to pray for elected officials.

- www.nationaldayofprayer.org

- www.prayercaucus.com

- www.presidentialprayerteam.org

Truths to Treasure

"...Fear God. *Honor* the king."

−1 Peter 2:17 NKJV

FASCINATING FACT:
The king that Peter was referring to in 1 Peter 2:17 was Herod Agrippa I, a very corrupt and self-serving leader. He came to power in 37 A.D. During his reign he was forced to take sides in the struggle between Judaism and Christianity. To better himself politically, he sided with the Jews and became a bitter persecutor of Christians. Acts 12:1-3 records that Herod Agrippa I killed James, one of Jesus' three closest disciples, and he seized Peter with the intention of killing him. (Page 79)

16. God *does* bring correction and rebuke to civil leaders who are corrupt and immoral. **Read** the following passages and briefly describe in each situation who received the rebuke, who brought it and why was it needed.

2 Samuel 11; 12:1-15 – Nathan and David

_____

_____

_____

1 Kings 16:29-33; 21:1-26 – Elijah and Ahab

_____

_____

_____

Mark 6:17-20 – John the Baptist and Herod

_____

_____

_____

17. God is the One who selects the person who will represent Him and deliver His warning of judgment to civil leaders. It will be firm, but it will also be done with respect.

a. When God *wants* you to say something to someone, how do you usually feel about it?

_____

_____

_____

_____

b. When God *doesn't* want you to say something to someone, how do you usually feel about it?

_____

_____

_____

_____

Check out
Ephesians
4:15 and 2
Chronicles
19:8,9

c. If God does choose you to be His mouthpiece to a civil leader, how does He want you to speak the truth to them?

_____

_____

_____

INSTANT *Replay*

*"Often we convey honor through financially giving. Recall, honor is to **value**. We put our finances in what we value."*
—John Bevere (Page 71)

18.   We invest our time, attention and money in the things we **value**. How valuable are your civil leaders to you? What would your life and the life of your children and/or grandchildren be like *without* policemen and firemen? What would your state be like *without* senators, representatives, judges or a governor?

_____

_____

_____

_____

_____

_____

_____

DIG Deeper

An attitude of honor and love for our leaders opens the door for God to speak truth into their lives. It builds a bridge between believers and unsaved civil leaders.

GET CREATIVE! In what practical ways can you begin to honor the civil leaders in your community? How can you specifically, and purposely, express honor, appreciation, respect and value for your firemen, policemen, councilmen, district judges, congressmen, etc.?

IDEA STARTERS
*   Bake small baskets of homemade goodies, such as cookies, cupcakes, brownies or bread. Wrap them in colorful paper and deliver them with a thank you card.

*   Buy a bunch of assorted candy bars and energy bars. Place them in a medium-sized box decorated by your children or children in your church with their pictures and handwritten messages from them saying, "Thanks for keeping us safe!"

- Find some fresh, colorful flowers or pretty potted plants, attach a card of encouragement and appreciation, and send it to some of the ladies serving as civil leaders.

I will bless and honor my civil leaders by...
(Pray and ask the Holy Spirit to show you how you can best honor and bless *your* civil leaders.)

_____

_____

_____

_____

_____

_____

CIVIL LEADERS I CAN HONOR
Jot down names and/or addresses of your leaders so that you can pray for them and bless them.
- My local FIRE department: _____
- My local POLICE precinct: _____
- My CITY COUNCILMAN: _____
- My MAYOR: _____
- My DISTRICT JUDGE: _____
- My STATE REPRESENTATIVE: _____
- My STATE SENATOR: _____
- My GOVERNOR: _____
- My U.S. REPRESENTATIVE: _____
- My U.S. SENATORS: _____

Hide in Your Heart

HONOR PRINCIPLE 4
Civil leaders are God's servants—they are working for Him. Therefore, we must show them both honor and respect in our thoughts, words and deeds (see Romans 13:3-7).

DESTRUCTIVE OR CONSTRUCTIVE...THAT IS THE QUESTION

"Therefore encourage (admonish, exhort) one another and edify (**strengthen** and **build up**) one another...."
—1 Thessalonians 5:11 AMP

It is apparent from this week's session on honoring civil leaders that the Christian community as a whole has really fallen short in this area. Instead of honoring our civil leaders through prayer and action, most of us have a tendency to murmur and complain about them, mainly because we have not been taught differently.

The truth is, when it comes to honoring those in authority, we can either be destructive or constructive—we can either do things to tear down and weaken our leaders or do things to build and strengthen them. Read the following story and see where you fit in:

As I watched them tear a building down
A gang of men in a busy town
With a ho-heave-ho, and a lusty yell
They swung a beam and the side wall fell

I asked the foreman, "Are these men skilled,
And the men you'd hire if you wanted to build?"
He gave a laugh and said, "No, indeed,
Just common labor is all I need."

"I can easily wreck in a day or two,
What builders have taken years to do."
And I thought to myself, as I went my way
Which of these roles have I tried to play?

Am I a builder who works with care,
Measuring life by rule and square?
Am I shaping my work to a well-made plan
Patiently doing the best I can?

Or am I a wrecker who walks to town
Content with the labor of tearing down?
"O Lord let my life and my labors be
That which will build for eternity!"[5]

We believe it is safe to say that all of us have dishonored our civil leaders in some way at some point in the past. Therefore, the first step toward honoring our civil leaders is the step of *repentance*. It is the foundation of growing in Christ and building for a better tomorrow.

The word *repent*, in the original Greek language, means "to change one's mind," always implying a change for the better. **Write out** and **take to heart** the related power principle found in ...

1 John 1:9

_____
_____
_____
_____

Psalm 32:1,5

_____

_____

_____

_____

Prayer of Repentance

Father, I come before You and humbly ask You to forgive me for thinking and saying critical and judgmental things about my civil leaders. I did not realize that they are Your servants doing Your work. Please help me to quickly recognize the negative thoughts and accusations about my civil leaders that the enemy tries to get me to think and then speak. Help me to take the energy I would use to complain about them and use it to pray for them.

God, please give me eyes to see my civil leaders the way You see them—especially those who are making bad decisions. You know all the pressures they face and everything they experienced growing up as a child, including all the hurts and abuse they received that is causing them to make the decisions they are making.

Father, You are the great Creator of heaven and earth, and I ask You to loose Your creativity in me to discover ways that I can honor and bless my civil leaders. Thank You for forgiving me and setting me free from a critical, judgmental attitude toward my leaders. Thank You for helping me and Christians everywhere honor our civil leaders through prayer and action. In Jesus' name, Amen!

Ponder the Promise

"Guard your heart above all else, for it determines the course of your life."

—*Proverbs 4:23 NLT*

Once we come clean with Christ and choose to change our thinking regarding our civil leaders, it is crucial that we *guard our hearts and minds* from being re-infected by the negative opinion of others. This is especially true with regard to where we get our news. Here are some specific steps you can take:

WHO – Carefully and prayerfully select your sources of news on the TV, radio, Internet and newspaper. Seek to select sources that provide the most *accurate* and *truthful* (and if possible, biblical) information in a balanced way.

WHAT – What emotions get stirred up inside you when watching, listening to or reading a certain source of news? This includes radio and TV talk shows. If it is consistently negative feelings like anger, rage, resentment, criticism, hopelessness, defeat and fear, you probably want to consider trying another source.

WHEN – The time of day you watch, read or listen to the news is important. It is wise not to take in the news just before going to bed. If at all possible, give yourself some time to digest the information you just received and let it drive you to prayer.

HOW – It is really not necessary to watch, hear, or read the news three or four times a day. Once you have prayerfully and carefully selected your news sources, limit your time and exposure to them.

FIND A NEED AND FILL IT!

There are many pastors and congregations who desperately want to reach their communities for Christ and see their churches grow. Many have tried a number of different things to get people to come to their church but have largely been unsuccessful. Through passionate prayer and a Spirit-led plan of action, what once seemed impossible *is possible* through God's anointing. The pastor and congregation of the church in Adelaide, Australia and the U.S. Midwest experienced this firsthand, and you can too!

Pastors: If the strategy you have been using for years to reach the lost in your community has been producing little or no fruit, why not try something new? God has given you the position and power to teach your congregation about the need to honor our civil leaders and how to do it. Begin to pray for God to stir up your leaders and congregation to desire to honor your civil leaders, and ask Him for favor with your civil leaders to have time to meet with them and find out how your church can best meet a need within your community.

Christian leaders and church members: You can pray that God will give your pastor and church leaders an open mind and a desire to honor your civil leaders. You can ask God for favor to meet with them and share what you have learned through this session. Remember, you don't want to be pushy or try to pressure your pastor or church leaders to do anything. Be respectful. As you faithfully pray, God will open the door for you to meet with them and/or allow them to catch the vision of honoring civil leaders.

INSTANT *Replay*

"When God's people honor those in authority, pray for them,
and walk in obedience to the Word of the Lord, we will see great
outpourings of God's Spirit on our towns, cities and nations."
—John Bevere (page 82)

EXPRESS YOUR EXPERIENCE

In what ways has this chapter on honoring civil leaders impacted you? What principle is He persistently hammering home in your heart? What action(s) is the Holy Spirit asking you to take? Write down anything that He is showing you.

_____

_____

_____

_____

_____

_____

_____

_____

_____

_____

_____

_____

_____

_____

_____

_____

_____

_____

_____

_____

_____

_____

_____

_____

_____

_____

_____

(1) *The Founder's Almanac* (The Heritage Foundation: Washington, D.C. 2002) p. 157. (2) Quotes on *judgmentalism* (www.dailychristianquote.com, retrieved 7/24/07). (3) Illustrations on criticism, good quotes (www.bible.org/illus.php?topic_id=744, retrieved 7/25/07). (4) Inspirational quotes on *The Christian Life* (www.spurgeongems.org/iquotes, retrieved 7/25/07). (5) See note 3.

Notes

"The cost of true greatness is humble, selfless, sacrificial *service*. The Christian who desires to be great and first in the kingdom is the one who is willing to serve in the hard place, the uncomfortable place, the lonely place, the demanding place, the place where he is not appreciated and may even be persecuted. Knowing that time is short and eternity is long, he is willing to spend and be spent. He is willing to work for excellence without becoming proud, to withstand criticism without becoming bitter, to be misjudged without becoming defensive, and to withstand suffering without succumbing to self-pity."

–John MacArthur[1]

CHAPTER 5
HONORING SOCIAL LEADERS

Please refer to Chapter 8 in the *Honor's Reward* book along with Session 5 of the teaching series.

DISREPUTE and BLASPHEME
Disrepute means "the state of being held in low esteem by the public."
Blaspheme means "to treat God or sacred things disrespectfully."

—American Dictionary of the English Language, **Noah Webster 1828**

1. What happens when we, as believers, neglect to honor our employers, teachers and other social leaders?

_____
_____
_____
_____
_____
_____
_____

2. How has society treated the things of God disrespectfully? Name some of the specific consequences that have taken place.

_____
_____
_____
_____
_____
_____
_____

> ### Truths to Treasure
> "Let all who are under the yoke as bond servants (*employees, students, athletes*) esteem their own [personal] masters (*employers, teachers, coaches*) worthy of honor and fullest respect, so that the name of God and the teaching [about Him] may not be brought into **disrepute** and **blasphemed**."
> *—1 Timothy 6:1 AMP*
> *(Words in italics added for clarification and emphasis.)*

3.   Have you ever "hit it off" with someone initially, but when they found out you were a Christian they gave you the "cold shoulder"? How did you respond? Were you able to discover the cause for their aggravation and hurt? If so, what was it?

_____

_____

_____

_____

_____

_____

_____

_____

INSTANT Replay

"What we *live* speaks so much louder than what we speak."
—John Bevere (Page 86)

4.   Do you know someone at work who is a Christian and takes *company time* to tell others about Jesus? How are they viewed by your coworkers and your boss? What do you think they could do differently to be a witness for Christ and not steal time from the company?

_____

_____

_____

_____

_____

_____

_____

5.   How can you display an *honoring heart* toward your employer? How about toward your teacher or coach?

_____

_____

_____

_____

_____

_____

_____

6. Have you ever made a positive impact on an employer, teacher or coach? Describe it.

_____

_____

_____

_____

_____

7. There are many words we can use to describe the type of character that shows honor. What words would you use to describe good character in a person?

_____

_____

_____

_____

_____

_____

> ### Truths to Treasure
>
> "[Tell] bond servants to be submissive to their masters, to be pleasing and give satisfaction in every way. [Warn them] not to talk back or contradict, nor to steal by taking things of small value, but to prove themselves truly loyal and entirely reliable and faithful throughout, so that in everything they may be an ornament and do credit to the teaching [which is] from and about God our Savior."
> —*Titus 2:9,10 AMP*

8. The damage we can cause by *dishonoring* a social leader who doesn't know Jesus can be devastating. In what ways can you show honor and God's love to someone who has been hurt by the dishonoring behavior of another believer?

_____

_____

_____

_____

_____

_____

9. Most of us decorate a Christmas tree each year, and one of the things we hang on it is *ornaments*. Titus 2:10 says that by being loyal, reliable and faithful employees in everything we do, we are like *ornaments* to the teaching of the Good News. Describe in your own words what this means.

_____

_____

_____

_____

_____

INSTANT *Replay*

"We are never to back down from what God's Word states.
We are to stand firm. However, we are to correct those who are
in opposition with a meek and gentle spirit. If it is our bosses, coaches
or teachers, we are to live a Christlike example. If the opportunity
arises, then we are to open our mouths and speak the truth
with love and respect to our leaders."
—John Bevere (Page 90)

10. John shares a story about a college professor who was confrontational and difficult to deal with at times. In previous years, this professor had some bad experiences with a few students who claimed to be Christians but did not represent Christ in a very good way. With John, however, things turned out differently. By the end of the class, the professor had softened toward him.

> *Truths to Treasure*
>
> "Instead, we will *speak the truth in love*, growing in every way more and more like Christ, who is the head of his body, the church."
>
> *—Ephesians 4:15 NLT*

  a. What were the reasons for the professor's change of heart?

  _____

  _____

  _____

  _____

  b. Why do you think the professor chose *not* to grade John's paper?

  _____

  _____

  _____

  _____

11. **Write out** and **take to heart** the related power principle found in Proverbs 15:1.

  _____

  _____

  _____

  _____

LESSONS from LEADERS

"Nothing is won by force. I choose to be *gentle*. If I raise my voice may it be only in praise. If I clench my fist, may it be only in prayer. If I make a demand, may it be only of myself."

—Max Lucado[3]

12. What are the differences between a slave mind-set and a servant mind-set? Write them in the grid below.

SLAVE MIND-SET	SERVANT MIND-SET

13. **Write out** and **take to heart** the related power passage in **Colossians 3:22-24**.

_____

_____

_____

_____

_____

_____

_____

_____

_____

_____

_____

Truths to Treasure

"Slaves *(employees)*, obey your earthly masters *(employers or bosses)* with deep respect and fear. Serve them sincerely as you would serve Christ. Try to please them all the time, not just when they are watching you. As slaves of Christ, do the will of God with all your heart. Work with enthusiasm, as though you were working for the Lord rather than for people. Remember that the Lord will reward each one of us for the good we do...."

—Ephesians 6:5-8 NLT
(Words in italics added for clarification and emphasis.)

DIG Deeper

Have you ever heard the expression, "Go the extra mile"? It was actually started by Jesus. In one part of His unforgettable Sermon on the Mount, Jesus gave us instructions on how we are to act when we're treated unjustly and harshly by those in authority over us. It was during that time that He said, "If someone

Truths to Treasure

"If someone forces you to go one mile, go with him *two* miles."

—Matthew 5:41 NIV

forces you to go one mile, go with him *two*."

Ancient Persian law allowed postal carriers to compel private citizens to assist in carrying their loads, and the Romans were no different. Just as the Roman soldiers compelled Simon of Cyrene to carry Jesus' cross, Romans had the authority to command a Jew to go "a thousand paces," or one Roman mile, to assist them.[4] When Jesus said go *two* miles, He was challenging His followers, both then and now, to rise above what was required of them and walk in excellence and mercy.

In a similar way, your boss has the authority to ask you to do various tasks around the office. In situations like these, you have an incredible opportunity to make an indelible impact on him or her for Christ. How? By going the *extra mile* and doing more than he or she is asking you to do. In this way, you'll honor your social leader and open the door for God's love to capture their heart.

Prayer for Strength

Father, thank You for the privilege of being able to come to You in prayer. I know it's Your desire for me to honor my social leaders, including my boss. Lord, I want to go the extra mile and do more than he's asking me to do to bring You glory, but I can't do it without Your strength. Please help me go the extra mile and honor You by honoring him. Help me remain calm and do my job as if I were doing it for You. I claim _____ (your boss's name) for Your kingdom. Penetrate the hardness and hurts of his heart with Your love. Use my actions and words to draw him closer to You, and give me a plan to go the extra mile at work. I thank You for giving me joy and for allowing my life to make a difference in his life for all eternity. In Jesus' name, Amen.

IDEA STARTERS
- Make your work station/desk clean and straight at the end of every day.
- Clean and straighten a common area before or after work without being asked. (Example: copy room, tool/storage area, kitchen/lunchroom)
- Tackle a job or project that needs to be done but no one else is willing to do.
- Work through lunch, come in early or stay late to finish a hot project.

My plan to "go the extra mile" at work is...

_____

_____

_____

_____

_____

_____

INSTANT Replay

"It is a law. If you honor the social authorities in your life, God *will* honor you, and you will be *fully rewarded*. It may not come from your boss, teacher or coach, but it will come. God is watching over His Word to perform it." (See Jeremiah 1:12.)
—John Bevere (Page 92)

THE WITNESS OF OUR LIPS AND OUR LIFE

"But in your hearts set Christ apart as holy [and acknowledge Him] as Lord. *Always be ready to give a logical defense* to anyone who asks you to account for the hope that is in you, but do it *courteously and respectfully*."
—1 Peter 3:15 AMP

Do you remember when you first learned about Jesus? More than likely, you heard the message of the Gospel more than once and from more than one person. Whatever the case, someone *witnessed* to you and told you about the great love of God and the greatest gift ever given—His Son, Jesus Christ. Take a few moments and reflect on that special time and then answer the questions below.

> ### Hide in Your Heart
>
> **HONOR PRINCIPLE 5**
> *Social leaders* are those who are in authority in public settings, such as employers, teachers, coaches, etc. God's Word declares that we are to honor and respect them, and in doing so God's name will be protected from being blasphemed in the community (see 1 Timothy 6:1).

Who influenced your life for Christ before you accepted Him as your Lord and Savior? What was it about their *character* that touched you the most?

_____

_____

_____

_____

Before you got saved, do you remember any Christians who *turned you off* from accepting Christ? What was it about their character that irritated and angered you the most? What can you learn from that experience and apply to your life today?

_____

_____

_____

_____

_____

The truth that others shared with you was very important, but the *way* they shared it was equally significant. As 1 Peter 3:15 says, when we share the Gospel and give a reason for the hope that is in us, we must do it *courteously* and *respectfully*.

Write out and **take to heart** the related power principles in these Scripture verses:

Also Check out Psalm 15:1-3; 39:1

Psalm 141:3

_____

_____

_____

Also Check out Proverbs 21:23

Proverbs 13:3

_____

_____

_____

Ponder the Promises

"Out of respect for Christ, be courteously reverent to one another."
—*Ephesians 5:21 The Message*

"Live creatively, friends. If someone falls into sin, forgivingly restore him, saving your critical comments for yourself. You might be needing forgiveness before the day's out."
—*Galatians 6:1 The Message*

2 Timothy 2:24-26

_____

_____

_____

_____

Even with fellow believers, we are to speak courteously and respectfully.

The "Wonder-Twin" Powers of Witnessing

As we have seen throughout this session, you and I do as much witnessing with our *lives* as with our lips. In fact, it is the witness of our lives that either closes or opens the door for the witness of our lips to be heard. At work, in the classroom, on the field or wherever we are, there are two qualities that cause us to really stand out—**excellence** and **integrity**.

It was a spirit of *excellence* that made Daniel stand out among all the other wise men of the land. His reputation paved the way for him to be able to speak into the life of the evil king of Babylon. Indeed, King Belshazzar himself said to Daniel, "I have heard of you, that the Spirit of God is in you, and that light and understanding and excellent wisdom are found in you" (Daniel 5:14 NKJV). The Bible goes on to say that "...Daniel was distinguished above the presidents and the satraps because an *excellent spirit* was in him, and the king thought to set him over the whole realm" (Daniel 6:3 AMP).

EXCELLENCE

The state of possessing good qualities in an unusual or eminent degree; the state of excelling in anything. To excel is 'to go beyond, to exceed, to surpass in good qualities or laudable deeds'.

– adapted from *American Dictionary of the English Language,* **Noah Webster 1828**

In what *practical* ways can your life show forth excellence?

_____
_____
_____
_____
_____
_____

Integrity and *excellence* go hand-in-hand. Integrity is not a *single* action but a pattern of actions consistently carried out in every area of a person's life. **Read** what John C. Maxwell, one of today's experts on the subject of leadership, has to say about integrity:

> "...In the midst of an ever-changing, often uncertain environment, there is one thing you have absolute control over—your integrity. When it comes to being honest, principled and ethical, you are the master of your own destiny. Other people and external forces might test it in various ways, but at the end of the day, you alone control your integrity.
>
> Integrity is all-encompassing. It's not something you demonstrate at home or church and set on a shelf at work. People

of integrity don't live separate lives; their morals, ethics, treatment of others and overall character are the same wherever they are, whatever they're doing.

When you follow the Golden Rule and live with integrity, you set an example that has a far greater impact than any words you could speak. Why is leading by example such a powerful concept? I can answer that with five short words: *People do what people see.*"[5]

Who do you know who lives a life of integrity?

_____

_____

_____

What is it about the way they live that exemplifies integrity? What characteristics of Christ do you see in them?

_____

_____

_____

_____

_____

LESSONS from LEADERS

"Do the right thing. It will gratify some people and astonish the rest."

–*Mark Twain*[6]

_____

_____

_____

_____

_____

_____

_____

Prayer for Power

*Lord, give me the grace to live a life of excellence and integrity in all that I do. Help me to control what I say and how I say it. May my good attitude and actions not be like a light switch I turn on and off, but something I consistently do **all** the time. Your Word says, in John 15:5, that apart from You I can do nothing, but through the strength of Jesus, I can do all things (see Philippians 4:13). Thank You for giving me the strength I need to live right and speak right. I give You the glory and the credit for everything good that comes out of my life. In Jesus' name, Amen.*

EXPRESS YOUR EXPERIENCE

Take a few minutes to spiritually "digest" this week's session. What principle(s) has the Holy Spirit really made alive to you? What Scripture(s) stands out the most to you with regard to where you are in life? What else is the Holy Spirit speaking to your heart? Ask Him to make it clear and thank Him for leading and guiding you into all truth (see John 16:13).

_____

_____

_____

_____

_____

_____

_____

_____

_____

_____

_____

_____

_____

_____

_____

_____

_____

_____

_____

_____

_____

_____

_____

_____

_____

_____

_____

_____

_____

(1) Quotes on *Service and a Servant's Heart* (www.dailychristianquote.com, retrieved 8/4/07). (2) Quotes on *Developing Godly Character As Men and Women of God* (www.dailychristianquote.com, retrieved 8/4/07). (3) Ibid. (4) An Eye for an Eye, from *The Word in Life™ Study Bible*, copyright © 1993, 1996 by Thomas Nelson, Inc. Used by Permission, p. 1635. (5) *People Do What People See*, Dr. John C. Maxwell, *Enjoying Everyday Life* magazine, July 2007, Joyce Meyer Ministries, Inc., Fenton, MO) p. 11. (6) See note 5, page 23.

"Let's again recap the meaning of honor. It is *to value, to esteem, to respect, to treat favorably,* and *to have high regard for.* If we are honoring our parents, we will communicate to them both verbally and through our body language with love and respect."

–*John Bevere*
Session 6

6 HONORING DOMESTIC LEADERS

Please refer to Chapter 9 in the *Honor's Reward* book along with Session 6 of the teaching series.

DISHONOR

To stain the character of; to lessen reputation; to disgrace, to bring shame or reproach (*criticism, condemnation, the act of despising*) on.

—American Dictionary of the English Language, **Noah Webster 1828**
(Italic words added to show clarification)

INSTANT Replay

"To honor our parents is not a suggestion, nor a recommendation; rather, it's a *commandment*."
—John Bevere (Page 93)

1. What are the *two* rewards promised to those who honor their father and mother?

_____

_____

_____

_____

Hide in Your Heart

HONOR PRINCIPLE 6
"Honor your father and mother," which is the first commandment with promise: "that it may be well with you and you may live long on the earth."
—Ephesians 6:2,3 NKJV

2. *Honor your father and mother* is actually the first commandment given by God to Moses and the children of Israel. **Write out** and **take to heart** the first appearance of this instruction found in Exodus 20:12.

_____

_____

_____

3. On what *one* condition does a child have the right *not* to submit to and obey his parents?

_____

_____

_____

4. What is keeping God's commandments evidence of? **Write out** and **take to heart** the related power principles found in John 14:21 and 2 John 6.

_____

_____

_____

_____

_____

Truths to Treasure

"God's curse *[is]* on anyone who demeans a parent. All respond: *Yes. Absolutely.*"
—Deuteronomy 27:16
The Message

INSTANT Replay

"You've got to remember this: The curse of God does not always show up right away. As a matter of fact, most of the time in the Scriptures, it shows up *later.*"
—John Bevere (Teaching from Session 6)

5. God gives a cataclysmic consequence to all who *dishonor* their father and mother. **Write out** and **take to heart** His powerful proclamation in Deuteronomy 27:16.

_____

_____

_____

_____

Check out
Genesis
9:20-27

6. One vivid example of a man who *dishonored* his father is Noah's youngest son Ham. He entered the tent where Noah lay drunk and naked and then went out and told his brothers about it.

a. What happened to Ham as a result of his behavior? Who was affected the most?

_____

_____

_____

b. How did Ham's brothers, Shem and Japheth, react? What did Noah do in response to their action?

_____

_____

_____

_____

_____

c. **Write out** and **take to heart** the related power principles Shem and Japheth demonstrated.

Proverbs 17:9 _____

_____

_____

_____

1 Peter 4:8 _____

_____

_____

_____

7. One of the greatest temptations we face when a person in authority messes up is to open our mouths and talk about it to others. We can be 100 percent right in our assessment of their wrong behavior, but 100 percent wrong in our *response*. What can you learn from this story about Ham in reference to your own experiences?

_____

_____

_____

_____

_____

_____

LESSONS from LEADERS

"Adults who did not receive a positive self-image from their fathers when they were children may feel insecure for a lifetime. Those who did receive positive, supportive messages from their dads will usually be strong even in the midst of adversity."

–Gary Chapman[1]

Truths to Treasure

"Every one of you shall *revere* his mother and his father..."

–Leviticus 19:3 NKJV

8. God tells us to honor our father and mother...

    a. when they honor and respect us and treat us right.
    b. until they ask us to do something that is directly against the Word of God.
    c. only if they humbly apologize for the wrong way they have treated us.
    d. regardless of how good or bad they are in our eyes or how honorable or dishonorable their behavior is.

9. Out of anger and hurt, have you ever done anything to your mother or father to get back at them for the way they treated you? If so, what was it?

    _____
    _____
    _____
    _____
    _____
    _____
    _____
    _____
    _____

10. Have you asked God to forgive you for dishonoring them? Are you still holding on to the hurt(s) or have you released it into God's hands? (We encourage you to refer back to the devotional *Freedom Through Forgiveness* in Chapter 3 of this workbook.)

    _____
    _____
    _____
    _____
    _____
    _____
    _____
    _____
    _____

LESSONS from LEADERS

"The greatest thing a father can do for his children is to love their mother. And the greatest thing a mother can do for her children is to love their father."

—*Josh McDowell*[2]

INSTANT Replay

"The husband is the head of the home. Chauvinistic
men didn't conjure this up; it is God's idea.
It is impossible to have true peace and blessing
in a home where a wife leads or dominates—where
the husband is not respected as the head."
—John Bevere (Pages 106-107)

11. What happens when a woman of God honors
her husband as the leader of the home?

_____

_____

_____

_____

_____

_____

_____

_____

_____

12. As a *wife*, how do you normally respond when your husband
has made a decision that you don't agree with? If you feel in
your heart his decision is wrong, what is the best thing you can
do? Is there anything God is showing you that you need to
change about the way you treat your husband?

_____

_____

_____

_____

_____

_____

_____

_____

_____

_____

_____

_____

13.   Scriptures like Ephesians 5:33 and Colossians 3:18, instructing wives to honor and submit to their husbands, certainly fly in the face of the philosophy that abounds in the popular culture today. Nevertheless, God's Word is *true* and doesn't change with culture. If a woman dishonors her husband and rebels against his authority, she will lose her reward and open the door for deadly problems to enter her life and the lives of her children.

      a.   Does your view reflect popular culture or the Word of God when it comes to honoring and submitting to your husband? Why?

_____

_____

_____

_____

_____

_____

_____

_____

      b.   What influences in your life *encourage* you to honor and submit to your husband?

_____

_____

_____

_____

_____

_____

_____

_____

_____

INSTANT Replay

"We are instructed to honor—not just for the sake of
those we honor, but for *us* as well. *We personally lose*
if we withhold honor from whom honor is due."

—John Bevere (Page 109)

John mentions that there are a number of popular "family movies" he couldn't let his children watch. Although the story lines were often touching, the children in the movies treated their mother and father as stupid and out of touch; they were disrespectful and blatantly disregarded their parents' instruction. Yet, in the end, these same children ended up as the heroes.

Unfortunately, there is an abundance of this kind of "entertainment" available—not only in movies but also on television, in video games, in music and other places. As parents, we have the God-given task of monitoring the media our children are *feeding* on. Just as a steady diet of the wrong foods will affect us *physically*, a steady diet of the wrong entertainment will affect us *spiritually*.

Ponder the Promises

"For as [a man] thinks in his **heart**, so is he...."
—Proverbs 23:7 NKJV

"A good man out of the good treasure of his **heart** brings forth good; and an evil man out of the evil treasure of his **heart** brings forth evil. For out of the *abundance* of the **heart** his mouth speaks."
—Luke 6:45 NKJV

"Guard your **heart** above all else, for *it determines the course of your life.*"
—Proverbs 4:23 NLT

In all these verses, the word *heart* refers to our inner man, the core of who we are—it includes our mind, will and emotions. Therefore, in order to protect your children from entertainment that can pollute and poison their hearts, pray (together as parents if possible) and ask the Lord to show you any movies, music, magazines, video games, TV shows, etc. that you need to remove from your *media menu.*

Here are some helpful questions to ask yourself: *Is what we're watching, reading and listening to showing disrespect and dishonor toward parents and those in authority? Is it benefiting our walk with God and increasing our love for others? Is this the kind of behavior I want to see in myself, my spouse and my children? What kind of effects is it having on me and my family—does it cultivate the fruit of God's Spirit or the desires of my flesh?* (See Galatians 5:19-23.)

The Lord is showing us (me) to get rid of these MOVIES, MUSIC CDS, MAGAZINES, ETC.:

1. _____
2. _____
3. _____
4. _____
5. _____
6. _____
7. _____

We feel it's best for our family to stop watching and listening to these TV SHOWS AND RADIO STATIONS:

1. _____
2. _____
3. _____
4. _____
5. _____
6. _____
7. _____

Check out the related power promise in Mark 10:29,30

As you *prayerfully* purge your media menu of impure things, ask the Lord to provide you and your family with a new selection of entertainment that is fresh, exciting and more interesting than ever!

PROCLAIMING AND CLAIMING GOD'S PROMISES

"Then said the Lord to me, 'You have seen well, for I am alert and active, *watching over My word to perform it.*'"

—Jeremiah 1:12 AMP

Promises, promises. God's Word is full of them, yet so many Christians fail to experience the reality of them in their lives, including the rewards of honoring their father and mother. Why is this? To a great degree, it's because our minds and mouths are *not* in agreement with God's Word. Instead, they are in agreement with the way we feel and the difficult circumstances and situations in which we find ourselves.

Please understand: Situations, circumstances and feelings are constantly *changing*. God's Word, on the other hand, is *unchanging*. Psalm 119:89 NKJV says, "**Forever**, O Lord, Your word is settled in heaven," and Isaiah 40:8 NKJV declares that "...the word of our God stands **forever**." Jesus, Himself, proclaimed in three of the four Gospels that heaven and earth will pass away, but His words will **never** pass away (Matthew 24:35, Mark 13:31, Luke 21:33).

So God's Word is forever established *in heaven*—but the Scripture says nothing about earth. The only way God's Word is established on earth is through the prayers and proclamations of believers. This is why Jesus prayed to the Father in Matthew 6:10 NKJV, "Your kingdom come. Your *will* be done *on earth*, as it is in heaven." God's *will* is His **Word**. By Jesus praying this way, He demonstrated a powerful principle: In order for God's will, or His Word, to be established **on earth** as it is in heaven, we must *proclaim His promises out of our mouths.*

Charles Capps, author and well-known minister of the Gospel, had some wonderful things to say about God's creative power that is released through our words:

> When you study the life of Jesus, you will find several important facts that caused Him to overcome the world, the flesh and the devil. I will list a few:
> 1. He spent much time in prayer, but He never prayed the problem; He prayed the answer. *What God said is the answer.*
> 2. He spoke accurately, never crooked speech. His conversation always consisted of what God said.
> 3. He always spoke the end results, *not the problem.* Never did He confess *present circumstances.* He spoke the *desired results.*
> 4. He used the written Word to defeat Satan.

> The Word of God conceived in the heart, formed by the tongue, and spoken out of the mouth is creative power.[3]

This being said, it is very important that we base our lives *not* on what changes, but on the unchanging, everlasting truth of God's Word. In order to see His promises become a reality in our lives, we need to fill our *minds* and *mouths* with them on a regular basis. This means renewing our minds daily with His unchanging truth—meditating on and memorizing Scripture.[4]

> ### Ponder the Promise
>
> "I have set watchmen upon your walls, O Jerusalem, who will never hold their peace day or night; you who [are His servants and by your prayers] *put the Lord in remembrance [of His promises]*, keep not silence."
> —*Isaiah 62:6 AMP*

LESSONS from LEADERS

"We need to realize that the promises that overflow our Bibles will overflow into our own lives *only* when we appropriate them *through prayer.*"

—Jim Cymbala[5]

Write out and **take to heart** these power principles from God's Word:

PSALM 19:14 _____

_____

PROVERBS 18:20,21 _____

_____

EPHESIANS 4:29 _____

_____

Has God made a special promise to you and confirmed it through His Word, but it has not come to pass yet? What is it and what Scripture(s) is it based on?

_____

_____

_____

_____

God declares in His Word that as you *honor your father and mother*, it will be well with you and you will live long on the earth. *Proclaim* and *claim* this promise and all His promises by filling your mind and mouth with what matters most—His unchanging Word!

Prayer to Release God's Power

> *Father, thank You for the powerful truths You have taught me in this session. May they soak deep down into the soil of my soul. It is my heart's desire to honor my father and mother.*
>
> *I ask You to forgive me for dishonoring my parents in any of my thoughts, words or actions (repent of anything specific the Holy Spirit reveals to you). I release them for all unfair or abusive treatment toward me (again, speak out anything specific the Holy Spirit shows you). Cleanse me with the precious blood of Jesus, and give me the grace to honor my father and mother regardless of how they treat me. I can do all things through Your strength.*
>
> *Help me to fill my mind and my mouth with the riches of Your unchanging Word. And may all negative talk be far from me. This seems impossible to me, but Your Word says nothing is impossible with You!*
>
> *Thank You, God, for working a miracle in my mouth and in my life. In Jesus' name, Amen!*

EXPRESS YOUR EXPERIENCE

After completing this week's session, in what specific ways do you plan to honor your parents? What question hit home the hardest with you? In what areas do you feel you need to grow? Take time to write down any other insights the Holy Spirit is revealing to you.

(1) *Quotes on fathers, by fathers, for fathers etc.* (www.waldsfe.org/fathers/quotes.htm, retrieved 8/13/07). (2) Quotes on *marriage* (www.dailychristianquote.com, retrieved 8/10/07). (3) Charles Capps, *God's Creative Power Will Work for You* (Tulsa, OK: Harrison House, Inc. 1976) pp. 14,15. (4) See Romans 12:2; Ephesians 4:22-23. (5) Favorite quotes under Christian Helps (www.character-buildingforfamilies.com, retrieved 8/11/07).

"Nobody can do as much damage to the Church of God as the man who is *within its walls,* but not within its life."

–*Charles Spurgeon*[1]

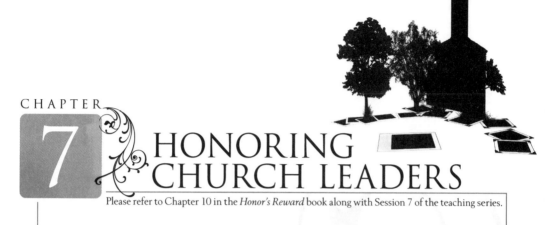

7 HONORING CHURCH LEADERS

Please refer to Chapter 10 in the *Honor's Reward* book along with Session 7 of the teaching series.

OFFENSE and SLANDER

To give **offense** means "to cause scandal or stumbling; to injure, attack or assault." To **slander** means "to defame; to injure by maliciously uttering a false report; to tarnish or impair the reputation of one by false tales."

– Adapted from *American Dictionary of the English Language,* **Noah Webster 1828**

INSTANT Replay

"In honoring a church leader we in turn honor Jesus,
and in honoring Jesus we honor God the Father (Matthew 10:40-41).
How we *act* toward, *speak* to, and even *think* of a leader is the way
we treat the One Who sent the leader. ...You cannot say you fear
God if you don't have respect for church authority."
—John Bevere (Page 110)

1. In the opening story, John shares a situation in which a man blatantly dishonored church authority. He goes on to explain that there are a number of believers who have the same root attitude; it is just more *subtle* and not as easily seen.

    a. Name three specific indications of subtle dishonor toward church leaders.

    _____

    _____

    _____

    _____

b. **Write out** Jesus' words of correction to the Pharisees in Matthew 15:7-9.

_____

_____

_____

_____

2. If your pastor asked everyone to attend a Friday night prayer meeting from 7 to 8 pm for four weeks and promised a $500,000 check for everyone who attends all four meetings, would you go?

> *Truths to Treasure*
>
> "*Obey* your spiritual leaders, and do what they say. Their work is to *watch over your souls*, and they are accountable to God...."
> *–Hebrews 13:17 NLT*

_____

_____

_____

_____

_____

_____

_____

_____

a. Would you attend *without* the promise of a check? Why did you answer the way you answered? (Remember, be honest with yourself and God. It's the key to being free.)

_____

_____

_____

_____

_____

_____

INSTANT *Replay*

"In 25 years of ministry...I've noticed the believers who are the most fulfilled, peaceful, happy, prosperous, and successful are those who *think highly* of and give *wholehearted* love and devotion to their church leaders."
—John Bevere (Pages 115-116)

3. Psalm 92:13 NKJV states that "those who are planted in the house of the Lord shall flourish in the courts of our God."

   a. Explain the difference between being *planted* in a local church and *attending* a local church, including advantages and disadvantages.

   _____
   _____
   _____
   _____
   _____

   b. List some reasons why you think people refrain from being planted in a local church.

   _____
   _____
   _____
   _____
   _____

   c. Those who do not view their pastor and church leaders as a *gift* from God are vulnerable to what?

   _____
   _____
   _____
   _____
   _____

4. A person who sees himself or herself *as good as* or *better than* their pastor has a problem with *pride*. **Write out** and **take to heart** the word of warning in 1 Peter 5:5 against this deadly disease of the soul that was the cause for Lucifer's ousting from God's presence.

   > **LESSONS** *from* **LEADERS**
   > "Nothing sets a person so much out of the devil's reach as humility."
   > –*Jonathan Edwards*[2]

   _____
   _____
   _____
   _____
   _____
   _____

THE TEST OF HONOR

Take the test and see where you rank.

YES/NO   Do you view your pastor as someone who can be easily replaced or really no different than anyone else?

YES/NO   Do you see your pastor as someone who is inferior in intelligence?

YES/NO   Does your pastor have to prove himself to you before you believe and receive what he's saying?

YES/NO   Do you find yourself getting up to go to the restroom just as your pastor is beginning to speak?

YES/NO   Do you leave your cell phone on during church just in case someone calls?

YES/NO   Do you find yourself reading the church bulletin, a magazine or a book during your pastor's sermon?

If you answered "yes" to two or more of these questions, you are showing the subtle symptoms of a dishonoring heart toward church leaders.

LESSONS from LEADERS

"More churches have been destroyed by the *accuser of the brethren* and its *faultfinding* than by either immorality or misuse of church funds. So prevalent is this influence in our society that, among many, faultfinding has been elevated to the status of a 'ministry'!"

—*Francis Frangipane*[3]

5.   When you hear of a minister, pastor or priest falling into sin, how do you react? What emotions rise up inside you? **Write out** and **take to heart** the power principle in Galatians 6:1 that tells us how we're to respond. (Use *The Amplified Bible* if possible.)

_____

_____

_____

_____

6. When someone close slanders a brother or sister in Christ to us, they *poison* our opinion of them. This is especially true when the person they slander is a church leader.

    a. Has someone ever brought slander or offense about a church leader to you? How did you react, and how did you feel about the leader afterward?

    _____

    _____

    _____

    b. Have *you* ever slandered or repeated an offense about a church leader to someone you know? Explain the situation.

    _____

    _____

    _____

    c. Why do you think the cutting words about a church leader carry so much weight?

    _____

    _____

    _____

LESSONS *from* LEADERS

"Notice, we *never pray* for folks we *gossip* about, and we *never gossip* about the folks for whom we *pray*! For prayer is a great deterrent."

—*Leonard Ravenhill*[4]

---

7. Honoring our father and mother carries the two-fold reward of a *blessed* life and a *long* life (see Ephesians 6:2,3). This same principle applies to our *spiritual* father and mother—someone who has been very instrumental in teaching us the truths of God's Word and helping us grow up in the Christian faith.

    a. Who do you consider your spiritual father(s) and mother(s)?

    _____

    _____

    _____

> *Truths to Treasure*
>
> "You shall not go up and down as a dispenser of *gossip* and *scandal* among your people, nor shall you [secure yourself by false testimony or by silence and] endanger the life of your neighbor. I am the Lord."
>
> —*Leviticus 19:16 AMP*

b. How *have* you honored them, or how *can* you honor them?

_____

_____

_____

c. Have you ever dishonored them? Describe the situation.

_____

_____

_____

d. Have you asked God to forgive you? Have you made restitution with them?

_____

_____

_____

INSTANT Replay

"Remember, God says we come under a *curse* when we dishonor
our father. Not only does this apply to our natural fathers, but
spiritual fathers as well. I personally believe a lot of tragic mishaps
could have been avoided if those involved would have developed
true honor within their hearts and guarded themselves from offense,
especially in regard to their spiritual fathers and mothers."

—John Bevere (Page 120)

Truths to Treasure

"Do not receive an
accusation against an
elder except from two
or three *witnesses*."
  —1 Timothy 5:19 NKJV

8. When we receive an accusation against our pastor or a church leader, it should only be received when it's presented by *two* or *three* **witnesses**. In this case, a *witness* is one who...

a. states the *exact* same story that some-one else is stating.

b. tells the message of the Gospel with a *sincere* heart.

c. carefully crafts a story about someone and finds others who will *testify* to its validity.

d. has *irrefutable* evidence that could stand up in a court of law.

INSTANT *Replay*

*"If we believe a rumor about a leader, it opens the door
to suspicion or inaccurate belief. Dishonor easily enters our hearts.
If we dishonor the leader, we can no longer receive the reward
God has to give us through that leader. ...All leaders carry a reward
from heaven. I personally don't want to miss a thing God
has for me, and I believe you feel the same way."*

—John Bevere (Pages 124-125)

DIG Deeper

In the last 15 to 20 years, there have been a number of church leaders who have fallen into sin and been objects of scandal. These scandals have cultivated the rapid spread of suspicion in the hearts and minds of multitudes in and outside the church.

Once we swallow the first bite of the *Bait of Satan*—offense or slander—it's much easier to swallow more. And the enemy is eagerly on task to furiously feed us as much as we'll take in. Many times we get so caught up in the *twister of tale bearing* that we repeat things to others without thinking—things we don't even know to be true. These are the *seeds of discord* that we talked about in Chapter 4—one of the seven things God hates. (See Proverbs 6:16-19.)

If you find yourself in the middle of this kind of mess, the first thing you need to do is repent for *receiving* and *sowing* seeds of slander, gossip and offense. Pray for a "crop failure" for all the seeds that have been sown in the soil of your soul and the souls of others. Then, ask the Lord to cover Christians everywhere with a healthy, holy reverential fear of Him.

Take a few minutes and write down the names of church leaders and fellow believers that come to mind about whom you have heard gossip, rumors or stories of offense. Also, include the names of those you have said or spread things about. These may be leaders in your church and denomination or in another church or

Ponder the Promise

"Love bears up under anything and everything that comes, is ever ready to believe the best of every person, its hopes are fadeless under all circumstances, and it endures everything [without weakening]."
–1 Corinthians 13:7 AMP

denomination. It may even be a well-known minister from television or radio. Here's a prayer to help you:

FATHER, PLEASE FORGIVE ME FOR *THINKING*, *SAYING* OR *RECEIVING* RUMORS, GOSSIP, SLANDER OR STORIES OF OFFENSE ABOUT CHURCH LEADERS.

_____
_____
_____
_____
_____
_____
_____

*Lord, whether what I thought, heard or said is true or not, I choose to let it go. You are the Judge, not me. Heal the hurt in my heart regarding what happened (tell the Lord anything specific that comes to mind). I will not curse_____ (person's name) any longer in my mind or with my mouth. Instead, I choose to **release** and **bless** _____(person's name) as Jesus instructed us to do in Luke 6:27,28. _____(person's name) doesn't owe me anything. Jesus paid the price for their sin and mine. And every time the enemy brings the memory of what _____ (person's name) did, I will **bless** them again, by Your grace. In Jesus' name, Amen!*

My Prayer of BLESSING for _____ **(person's name) is...**
Write down anything good that you would like to see happen in your life, and pray for it to happen in their life. This includes blessings in the physical, spiritual, financial, relational, and emotional areas of their life.

_____
_____
_____
_____
_____
_____
_____

"ORDER IN THE COURT!"

"It **isn't** my responsibility to judge *outsiders*, but it certainly is your responsibility to judge those *inside the church* who are sinning. God will judge those on the outside; but as the Scriptures say, 'You must remove the evil person from among you.'"

—1 Corinthians 5:12,13 NLT

If there has ever been an issue that has brought both confusion and frustration to believers, it is the subject of *judging*. Some believers feel that we are never to judge anyone or anything, while others have made it their "full-time ministry." What is the right answer?

Well, as 1 Corinthians 5:12,13 clearly states, it is *not* our responsibility to judge outsiders, or unbelievers—God will judge them (see Revelation 20:11-15). However, it *is* our responsibility to judge those *inside the church* who are sinning (and I emphasize, those who are sinning).

Paul vehemently warns us in 1 Corinthians 5:11 NLT that we "...are not to associate with anyone *who claims to be a **believer*** yet indulges in sexual sin, or is greedy, or worships idols, or is abusive, or is a drunkard, or cheats people. *Don't even eat with such people.*"

On the opposite end of the spectrum, we discover a Scripture like 1 Corinthians 4:5 NLT, which states "...*don't make judgments about anyone ahead of time—before the Lord returns. For he will bring our darkest secrets to light and will reveal our private* **motives**. *Then God will give to each one whatever praise is due.*"

So what's the difference between these two verses? The first deals with a believer's *actions*, and the second deals with a believer's *motives*. Actions are on the outside—they are a person's behavior that can clearly be seen by all. You and I *are* to judge a person's actions. This is what Jesus meant when He said, "You will know them by their **fruits**..." (Matthew 7:16 NKJV).

Why do you think we are to deal with believers who are blatantly involved in sin?

Check out
1 Corinthians
5:6,7 for help

_____

_____

_____

What are we to judge a person's actions against—what is the measuring rod, or standard, we are to use to know if a person is sinning?

_____

_____

INSTANT *Replay*

*"The love of God believes a person is innocent until proven guilty.
Cynical people believe people are guilty until proven innocent.
Which one are you?"*
—John Bevere (Teaching from Session 7)

Of course we are not to judge everything we see on the outside—only the *behavior* we know to be wrong. Even then we are to *act in love* and *the fear of the Lord* (see Galatians 6:1-4; Romans 15:1). **Read** this story and see if you can identify some things on the outside we are *not* to judge:

"Dodie Gadient, a schoolteacher for 13 years, decided to travel across America and see the sights she had taught about. Traveling alone in a truck with camper in tow, she launched out. One afternoon rounding a curve on I-5 near Sacramento in rush-hour traffic, a water pump blew on her truck. She was tired, exasperated, scared, and alone. In spite of the traffic jam she caused, no one seemed interested in helping.

Leaning up against the trailer, she prayed, 'Please God, send me an angel...preferably one with mechanical experience.' Within four minutes, a huge Harley drove up, ridden by an enormous man sporting long, black hair, a beard and tattooed arms. With an incredible air of confidence, he jumped off and, without even glancing at Dodie, went to work on the truck. Within another few minutes, he flagged down a larger truck, attached a tow chain to the frame of the disabled Chevy, and whisked the whole 56-foot rig off the freeway onto a side street, where he calmly continued to work on the water pump.

The intimidated schoolteacher was too dumbfounded to talk. Especially when she read the paralyzing words on the back of his leather jacket: 'Hell's Angels—California.' As he finished the task, she finally got up the courage to say, 'Thanks so much,' and carry on a brief conversation. Noticing her surprise at the whole ordeal, he looked her straight in the eye and mumbled, 'Don't judge a book by its cover. You may not know who you're talking to.' With that, he smiled, closed the hood of the truck, and straddled his Harley. With a wave, he was gone as fast as he had appeared."[5]

After reading Dodie's story, what are some of the things on the outside that we are **not** to judge?

_____

_____

_____

_____

Has a situation like Dodie's ever happened to you? Describe what took place and what you learned.

_____

_____

_____

_____

_____

_____

_____

_____

_____

_____

> ### LESSONS from LEADERS
> "If you *judge* people, you have no time to *love* them."
>
> —*Mother Teresa*[6]

MEDITATE ON THE MESSAGE

In a nutshell, we are *not* to judge outsiders, or unbelievers—that's God's job. We *are* to judge a man's actions, or fruits, but we are to do so *in love* with the hope of seeing him repent and restored to a right relationship with the Father. Remember, love covers—it does not expose a man's sin for all to see. So keep your mind and mouth free from gossip and slander.

When it comes to a person's motives, they too are to be judged by God and God alone. Only He can measure them accurately. Motives are on the *inside*—they are the *reasons for our actions* and are not clear for all to see. **Take to heart** these related power principles from God's Word:

> ### LESSONS from LEADERS
> "He who is filled with *love* is filled with God himself."
>
> —*Saint Augustine*[7]

Ponder the Promises

"...'Don't judge by his appearance or height, for I have rejected him. The LORD doesn't see things the way you see them. People judge by outward appearance, but the LORD looks at the heart.'"

—*1 Samuel 16:7 NLT*

"...Give what each deserves, for you know each life from the inside (you're the only one with such 'inside knowledge'!)...."

—*1 Kings 8:39 The Message*

"...For the LORD searches every heart and understands every motive behind the thoughts...."

—*1 Chronicles 28:9 NIV*

"We may think we know what is right, but the LORD is the judge of our motives."

—*Proverbs 16:2 CEV*

EXPRESS YOUR EXPERIENCE

What about this session on honoring church leaders impacted you the most? In what area(s) do you feel the Lord is asking you to come up higher? Get quiet and take a few moments to write down any specific things the Holy Spirit is showing you or asking you to do.

_____

_____

_____

_____

_____

_____

_____

_____

_____

_____

_____

_____

_____

_____

_____

_____

_____

_____

_____

_____

_____

_____

_____

_____

_____

_____

_____

_____

_____

_____

_____

_____

_____

(1) Quote by Charles Spurgeon (www.characterbuildingforfamilies.com/quotes.html, retrieved 8/16/07). (2) Quotes on *Pride and Humility* (www.dailychristianquote.com, retrieved 8/15/07). (3) Quotes on *Gossip and Taming the Tongue* (www.dailychristianquote.com, retrieved 8/15/07). (4) Ibid. (5) Illustrations on *Judging* (www.sermonillustrations.com, retrieved 8/16/07). (6) Quotes on *Spiritual Development* (www.motivational-inspirational-corner.com/getquote.html, retrieved 8/16/07). (7) Ibid.

Notes

"There are three
conversions necessary:
the conversion of
the heart, mind,
and the *purse.*"

–Martin Luther[1]

BANK

8

DOUBLE HONOR

Please refer to Chapter 11 in the *Honor's Reward* book, along with session 8 of the teaching series.

FIRST FRUITS

The fruit or produce first matured and collected in any season. Of these the Jews made an oblation (*offering or sacrifice*) to God, as acknowledgement of His sovereign dominion; the first profits of anything. (Note: The Hebrew word translated first fruits in Proverbs 3:9 means the "chief" or "principal part.")[2]

– *American Dictionary of the English Language,* **Noah Webster 1828**
(Words in italics added for clarity; footnote applies to note only.)

1. Why is 1 Timothy 5:17 significant in regards to giving honor to those in authority?

   _____
   _____
   _____

2. According to Ephesians 4:11, the fivefold forms of ministry, which include apostles, prophets, evangelists, pastors and teachers, are...

   a. powerful positions of church leadership that a person can attend seminary to achieve.
   b. characteristics each church leader must develop and operate in.
   c. given as gifts to us, the church, by Jesus Christ Himself.
   d. specifically linked to the early church and are not all still in operation today.

> **𝓗ide in 𝓨our 𝓗eart**
>
> **HONOR PRINCIPLE 8**
> "Let the elders who rule well be counted worthy of double honor, especially those who labor in the word and doctrine (preaching and teaching). For the Scripture says, 'You shall not muzzle an ox while it treads out the grain,' and, 'The laborer is worthy of his wages.'"
> –*1 Timothy 5:17,18 NKJV*
> (*Words in parentheses added for clarity.*)

3. List *five* or more **practical ways** you can give your Christian leaders double honor.

_____

_____

_____

_____

_____

_____

_____

_____

TITHE

The tenth part of anything; but appropriately, the tenth part of the increase annually arising from the profits of land and stock, allotted to the clergy for their support.

— American Dictionary of the English Language, **Noah Webster 1828**

---

4. There are a number of people who believe tithing is an *Old Testament requirement* under the Law of Moses, and it does not apply to Christians today. But Jesus said He didn't come to abolish the Law but to *fulfill* it (see Matthew 5:17). He actually took the commandments of the Law and raised them to a higher standard under the Spirit.

    a. **Read** Genesis 14:1-20 and Hebrews 7:1-4. Briefly **write out** the account of this father of our faith who tithed to the Lord *before* the Law was even given.

> *Truths to Treasure*
>
> "'Bring all the tithes into the storehouse so there will be enough food in my Temple. If you do,' says the LORD of Heaven's Armies, 'I will open the windows of heaven for you. I will pour out a blessing so great you won't have enough room to take it in! Try it! *Put me to the test!*'"
>
> *—Malachi 3:10 NLT*

_____

_____

_____

_____

b. What other prominent player in God's family committed to
tithe to God *before* the Law was given to Moses and the
Israelites?

       Check out
       Genesis
       28:20-22

_____

_____

_____

_____

c. **Read** what Jesus said to the scribes and Pharisees in
Matthew 23:23 and Luke 11:42 about tithing. Does He do
away with or endorse tithing?

_____

_____

_____

_____

d. **Check out** what Jesus said in Matthew 5:21,22,27,28
concerning the commandments on murder and adultery. In
light of His response, what do you think He might say to you
and me today about tithing?

_____

_____

_____

_____

LESSONS *from* LEADERS

"The tithe was established as a physical, earthly demonstration of man's commitment to God. God understood our greedy, selfish nature and provided an identifiable sign of our sincerity."

—Larry Burkett[3]

INSTANT *Replay*

"In the ministry down through the years and in the Bible
there has been abuse to the honor principle; but we must ask,
should this abuse cause us to veer away from the *scriptural
command* of giving double financial honor to God's servants?
Two wrongs have never made a right in God's eyes."
—John Bevere (Page 133)

5.   It has often been said, "The Gospel is preached freely, but it's
     not freely preached." In other words, it costs money to fulfill the
     Great Commission and proclaim the Good News to all the
     nations of the world.

     a.   What do you think causes people to cringe when it comes
          to offering time?

          _____

          _____

          _____

          _____

     b.   What emotions rise up in *you* when you are asked to give?

          _____

          _____

          _____

          _____

     c.   Do you give tithes? Do you give offerings? Why or why not?
          Get quiet before the Lord and ask Him to show you your
          heart.

          _____

          _____

          _____

          _____

6.   According to Scriptures like Malachi 3:10 and Proverbs 3:9, we
     are to honor God by giving Him a portion of our money—tithes
     and offerings. But you and I can't *physically* give God money. So
     what are we supposed to do?

     _____

     _____

     _____

     _____

     _____

INSTANT Replay

"When we withhold the tithe or offerings from those God sends us,
we harm only *ourselves* because we dishonor the Lord."
—John Bevere (Page 144)

7. Second Peter 1:21 NKJV states that "...prophecy never came by the will of man, but holy men of God spoke *as they were moved by the Holy Spirit.*" With this in mind, Paul's instruction to financially give Christian leaders *double honor* was straight from the heart of God. When we disobey this command, we close the door on God's blessings and open the door to the enemy's curse.

a. What kinds of *problems* have you seen that typically abound in churches that *don't* pay their pastors well?

_____

_____

_____

_____

_____

b. What kinds of *blessings* have you seen that typically abound in churches that *do* pay their pastors well?

_____

_____

_____

_____

> ### Truths to Treasure
>
> "Should people *cheat* God? Yet you have cheated me! But you ask, 'What do you mean? When did we ever cheat you?' You have cheated me of the *tithes* and *offerings* due to me. You are under a curse, for your whole nation has been cheating me."
>
> *—Malachi 3:8,9 NLT*

LESSONS from LEADERS

"When a church seeks a *pastor*, they want the strength of an eagle, the grace of a swan, the gentleness of a dove, the friendliness of a sparrow, and the night hours of an owl. And when they catch that bird, they expect the pastor *to live on the food of a canary.*"

—Anonymous4

8. John shared a powerful story about a church he visited where the people weren't properly caring for their pastor financially. As a result, the church had not grown in size for years and there was no evident move of God's power and presence. John exposed the problem to the people and then honored the pastor and his wife by taking a special offering for them. Within less than a week, God began pouring out blessings on the church members.

a. In view of this story, how would you describe the health of your church?

_____

_____

_____

_____

b. Does your pastor's wife work outside the church because she wants to or she has to financially? Overall, how does your church take care of your pastor *financially*? Is there anything your church could do differently?

_____

_____

_____

_____

INSTANT Replay

"If you take the truths of this chapter and read the entire Bible, you'll notice whenever the people of God richly gave, miracles, freedom, salvations, God's presence, and prosperity would abound. We cannot buy the blessings of God; however, it is a spiritual principle God has weaved into His grace. ...By giving *double financial honor* to those who bring the Word of God to us, we position ourselves to be honored by God; included in that honor is grace and favor—it's a spiritual law."
—John Bevere (Page 146)

9. Jesus says, "He who receives you receives Me, and he who receives Me, receives Him who sent Me" (Matthew 10:40 NKJV). It's a spiritual fact: The way we treat those Jesus sends us is *exactly* how we treat Him and the Father in heaven.

a. So, how would you want Jesus to be treated if He *personally* was your pastor or if He visited your church to minister?

_____

_____

_____

_____

_____

b. What would you do differently than you are presently doing?

_____

_____

_____

10. Throughout Scripture we are instructed to give to God's servants who *teach, preach* and *serve* in His house. **Write out** and **take to heart** these New Testament power principles on giving.

Galatians 6:6 _____

_____

_____

1 Corinthians 9:14 _____

_____

_____

2 Corinthians 9:6,7 _____

_____

_____

LESSONS *from* LEADERS

"Givers can be divided into three types: the flint, the sponge and the honeycomb. Some givers are like a piece of flint—to get anything out of it you must hammer it, and even then you only get chips and sparks. Others are like a sponge—to get anything out of a sponge you must squeeze it and squeeze it hard, because the more you squeeze a sponge, the more you get. But others are like a honeycomb, which just overflows with its own sweetness. That is how God gives to us, and it is how we should give in turn."

—Anonymous[5]

---

11. When we put God first and are obedient and give as He instructs, He promises to faithfully provide for our needs. **Write out** and **take to heart** these related power *promises* from His Word.

Matthew 6:33 _____

_____

_____

_____

Luke 6:38 _____
_____
_____
_____

2 Corinthians 9:8 _____
_____
_____
_____

Philippians 4:19 _____
_____
_____
_____

12. If we are living a life of excellence by the grace of God, we are
going to be a blessing to others. As a result, people are going
to bless and honor us. What are we to do with the honor that
other people show to us?

_____
_____
_____
_____
_____

INSTANT Replay

"For a leader to *seek* or *demand* honor is out of step with the heart of
God. Jesus said, 'I crave no human honor' (John 5:41 AMP). He sought
only the honor that came from the Father. ...Jesus received honor from
men and women *for their sake,* and most of all for His Father's sake."
—John Bevere (Page 129)

Accept the challenge of Malachi 3:10! Put God to the
TEST! Don't give God your *leftovers*—give Him your
first fruits! **Check out** this insightful excerpt on giving
taken from *The Miracle of Malachi*, an article written
by Christian CPA and registered investment advisor
Bob Katz.

"After counseling hundreds of people over the last 30 years, I am convinced that one of the most powerful spiritual weapons we have against attacks on our finances is to be faithful with our *tithes* and *offerings*. Simply put, financial freedom comes as we learn to be extravagant givers.

The book of Malachi is one of the most powerful books in the Bible. In it the Lord is once again calling to His disobedient people. Over and over He says, 'Return to Me, and I will return to you.' And then He makes some unique statements and promises that are found nowhere else in Scripture. First, He bluntly tells His people they are robbing Him. How were they robbing God? By not giving their tithes and offerings. Of all the sins the Lord could have chosen—adultery, murder, worshipping false gods, etc.—His focus was on tithes and offerings.

The Lord then makes one of the most incredible statements I have ever read in Scripture—He says four words that are found nowhere else in the Bible: 'Test Me in this' (see Malachi 3:10). The command to be faithful with our tithes and offerings is so important to God that He asks us, His creation, to test Him, the Creator. Why? Clearly, He does not need our money. Why are tithes and offerings so important to the Lord? The reason is that He absolutely wants our **hearts**, and He knows that '...where [our] treasure is, there [our] heart will be also' (Matthew 6:21 NIV)."[6]

If you are not currently tithing, pray and ask God to give you the grace (strength and ability) to obey His Word and do so. Even if your income is small, develop a plan to work toward giving a tithe. If you need to, start giving $1 or $5 a week and then gradually increase the amount until you reach the full tithe (10 percent).

MY PLAN TO TITHE: _____

_____

_____

_____

_____

_____

_____

Ask God to show you where He would have you invest your resources and how much He would have you give beyond your tithe, in offerings. Remember, you can't "out-give" God. Give what you feel prompted by the Holy Spirit to give—not out of emotion or pressure.

MY PLAN TO GIVE OFFERINGS: _____

_____

_____

LESSONS from LEADERS

"Where your *pleasure* is, there is your treasure; where your *treasure* is, there is your heart; where your *heart* is, there is your *happiness*."

—*St. Augustine*[7]

God will honor your efforts to give your tithes and offerings—He will be faithful to keep His Word to provide for your needs. **Meditate on the message** of these powerful promises declaring that God is a God Who keeps His Word.

Ponder these Promises

"The words and promises of the Lord are pure words, like silver refined in an earthen furnace, purified seven times over."

—*Psalm 12:6 AMP*

"Israel's God-of-Glory doesn't deceive and he doesn't dither. He says what he means and means what he says."

—*1 Samuel 15:29 The Message*

"As for God, His way is perfect; the word of the Lord is *proven*; He is a shield to all who trust in Him."

—*2 Samuel 22:31 NKJV*

"God is not a man, that he should lie, nor a son of man, that he should change his mind. Does he speak and then not act? Does he promise and not fulfill?"

—*Numbers 23:19 NIV*

INSTANT Replay

"It never fails. If we will honor our spiritual leaders financially, we will prosper in our own lives."

—John Bevere (Page 136)

THE PROMISE OF HIS PRESENCE

"...In Your presence is fullness of joy; at Your right hand are pleasures forevermore."

—Psalm 16:11 NKJV

God's promise of financial provision to all who give to His work and His workers is absolutely awesome. It brings us security and peace of mind to know that when we obediently give our tithes and offerings, He will make sure that we *always* have what we need—and more to give.

However, an even greater blessing than financial provision is promised. Proverbs 3:9,10 NKJV declares, "Honor the LORD with your possessions, and with the firstfruits of all your increase; so your *barns* will be filled with plenty, and your *vats* will overflow with new wine." As John explained, the word **barns** symbolizes your storage areas. These would include such things as your bank account or checkbook, which stores your money; your closets and dressers, which store your clothes; and your cupboard and refrigerator, which store your food.

The word **vat** is also very special. It refers to the storage bins of a wine press that hold the new wine after the grapes are crushed. *New wine* is a symbol of the fresh presence of the Holy Spirit. So when the Scripture says our vats will overflow with new wine when we honor the Lord with our first fruits, it means our lives will overflow with the fresh presence of the Holy Spirit!

In God's presence is *everything* we need. Ephesians 1:3 NKJV says, "Blessed be the God and Father of our Lord Jesus Christ, who has blessed us with *every spiritual blessing* in the heavenly places in Christ." With the blessing of God's presence come joy, peace, power, favor, revelation of His Word, and every other good thing we could ever need or want.

God communicates a similar message in Malachi 3:10 NASB, promising to open "...the *windows of heaven* and pour out for you a blessing until it *overflows.*" It's true that this includes the provisions we need, but it is so much more than that. Think about it. What do you do at a window? You *look* through it. By God saying He will open the windows of heaven, He is saying we can see into the heart of where He lives, gaining understand-

> ## LESSONS from LEADERS
>
> "A believer longs after God—to come into His **presence**...to feel His love...to feel near to Him in secret...to feel in the crowd that He is nearer than all the creatures. Ah! Dear brethren, have you ever *tasted* this blessedness? There is greater rest and solace to be found *in the presence of God* for one hour, than in an eternity of the presence of man.
>
> —*Robert Murray M'Cheyne*[8]

ing, revelation and answers to life's issues. Without question, an overflow of this nature—God's presence, which includes His wisdom and all that He is—is uncontainable!

Moses knew the incomparable value of God's presence. **Write out** and **take to heart** his prayer for God's presence found in Exodus 33:14,15.

_____

_____

_____

_____

_____

David also greatly appreciated and pursued the presence of the Father. **Write out** and **take to heart** his cry for God's presence in Psalm 27:4.

_____

_____

_____

_____

_____

Ponder the Promise

"O **taste and see** that the Lord [our God] is good! Blessed (happy, fortunate, to be envied) is the man who *trusts* and *takes refuge* in Him."
—*Psalm 34:8 AMP*

Have you "tasted" of the Lord's presence? If so, how would you describe it? How valuable is God's presence to you?

_____

_____

_____

_____

_____

_____

Have you ever been in the flow of fellowship with the Father and something happened to interrupt it? Describe your experience.

_____

_____

_____

_____

_____

Rest assured, when you honor church leaders by tithing, giving offerings as well as giving into their lives personally, you will receive the *full reward* of the overflow of God's presence!

INSTANT *Replay*

"There is nothing greater than having an over abundance—more than you can contain—of [God's] presence. [It] is the greatest reward you can give any person for honoring God with their finances."
—John Bevere (Teaching from Session 8)

Prayer

Father, thank You so much for this eye-opening teaching on giving to church leaders. May the truths and principles I have discovered be indelibly imprinted within my soul and spirit to such a degree that they show up in my actions.

I ask You to forgive me for withholding any tithes or offerings from You. Help me to hear Your voice clearly when You ask me to give to my church and other ministries You want me to invest in. Please take away my fears of running out of resources; help me to trust You to keep Your Word and live up to Your name—Jehovah Jireh, the Great Provider.

Father, I desire to seek Your face and not just Your hand—I want Your friendship more than what You can give me. I expect You to bless me with provisions, but more than that, I desire the blessing of Your overflowing presence in my life. I love You, Lord! In Jesus' name, Amen!

EXPRESS YOUR EXPERIENCE

How has this week's session impacted you? What new things did the Holy Spirit reveal to you? What were you reminded of that you had forgotten? In what ways are you challenged? Write down anything else the Holy Spirit is speaking to you.

_____
_____
_____
_____
_____
_____
_____
_____
_____
_____

_____
_____
_____
_____
_____
_____
_____
_____
_____
_____
_____
_____
_____
_____
_____
_____
_____
_____
_____
_____
_____
_____
_____
_____
_____
_____
_____
_____
_____
_____
_____
_____
_____
_____
_____
_____

(1) Quotes on *Stewardship, Tithing, Money and Finances* (www.dailychristianquote.com, retrieved 8/21/07). (2) *The New Unger's Bible Dictionary*, Merrill R. Unger, R. K. Harrison Editor (Moody Press: Chicago, IL 1988). (3) Larry Burkett, *Larry Burkett's Little Instruction Book on Managing Your Money* (Tulsa, OK: Honor Books, Inc., 1996) p. 109. (4) See note 1. (5) Ibid. (6) "The Miracle of Malachi," Bob Katz, *Enjoying Everyday Life* magazine, March 2006, Joyce Meyer Ministries, Inc., Fenton, MO). (7) See note 1. (8) Quotes on *Intimacy with God* (www.dailychristianquote.com, retrieved 8/22/07).

Notes

"How wonderful, how beautiful, when brothers and sisters get along! It's like costly anointing oil... It's like the dew on Mount Hermon flowing down the slopes of Zion. Yes, *that's where GOD commands the blessing,* ordains eternal life."

–King David
Psalm 133:1-3 The Message

9

HONORING OUR PEERS

Please refer to Chapter 12 in the *Honor's Reward* book along with Session 9 of the teaching series.

PEER

An equal; one of the *same* rank; a companion, a fellow, an associate.

– American Dictionary of the English Language, **Noah Webster 1828**

INSTANT *Replay*

"There are many people on our level. When we honor *people on our level,* they carry a certain reward."
—John Bevere (Teaching from Session 9)

> ### Truths to Treasure
>
> "...He who receives a *righteous man* in the name of a righteous man shall receive *a righteous man's reward.*"
> *—Matthew 10:41 NKJV*

1. Have you ever had a peer—someone on your level, a friend—do something to you that really hurt you and made you angry with them?

    _____

    _____

    a. Explain what happened and share how you worked through your feelings.

        _____

        _____

        _____

        _____

        _____

b. How did you respond to your peer and handle the situation?

_____

_____

_____

_____

_____

2. In the story about the pastor who hired one of John's workers out from under him, God prompted John to give something of great value to him. Name *three* specific, positive things that happened as a result of John's willingness and obedience to give the gift.

_____

_____

_____

_____

_____

3. Has the Lord ever prompted you to give something away or do something for a peer who hurt you? Did you do it? Describe the situation and the outcome.

_____

_____

_____

_____

_____

LESSONS from LEADERS

"Never let a problem to be solved become more important than a person to be loved."

–*Barbara Johnson*[1]

INSTANT Replay

"Confrontation is good, however it must be done with a right heart attitude. It must be done for the sake of the other person, not for us."

—John Bevere (Page 149)

4. In order to fully get over his anger and hurt, John also had to *confront* the pastor who had offended him. Confronting some one who hurt us is often scary or hard to do with a good attitude.

a. What was the *first* thing John did after he was hurt?

_____

_____

b. At what point did John confront the pastor? What had to happen first?

_____

_____

_____

_____

_____

c. What can you learn from this example and apply in your own life?

_____

_____

_____

_____

_____

5. By God's grace, John overcame the *wrong* (the hiring of one of his employees) by doing *good* (praying for the pastor, confronting him in love, and giving him his new watch). **Write out** and **take to heart** this clear demonstration of Romans 12:21, which echoes the instruction of Psalm 34:14.

_____

_____

_____

_____

_____

PRETENSE

Holding out or offering to others something *false* or feigned; a presenting to others, either in words or actions, a *false* or *hypocritical appearance*, usually with a view to conceal what is real, and thus to deceive.

– *American Dictionary of the English Language,* **Noah Webster 1828**

INSTANT Replay

"To extend true honor, it must be done *without* hypocrisy. It can never be done in *pretense*; it'll only lead to deception, and there's definitely no reward for the counterfeit."
—John Bevere (Page 153)

6. One of the most challenging things we face as believers is being *real* with one another—truthfully sharing with those on our level how we're feeling and expressing what's going on in our lives. Has this been a difficulty in your life? Why do you think this happens?

    _____

    _____

    _____

    _____

    _____

7. In your own words, describe what a *hypocrite* is. Have you ever been guilty of being a hypocrite? Explain the situation.

    _____

    _____

    _____

    _____

    _____

8. Did the scenario described between "Steve" and "Jim" in Chapter 12 sound familiar? Most of us have experienced situations like this.

    a. What does Steve's internal conversation possibly indicate about his relationship with Jim?

        _____

        _____

        _____

    _____

    _____

    _____

> *Truths to Treasure*
>
> "Let love be without *hypocrisy*. Abhor what is evil. Cling to what is good. Be kindly affectionate to one another with brotherly love, in *honor* giving *preference* to one another."
> —Romans 12:9,10 NKJV

    b. How could Steve have responded differently and yet been truthful?

        _____

        _____

        _____

        _____

        _____

INSTANT Replay

"When the *fear of God* is in you, you will not speak deceit; you will speak from your heart.... This is so important—we must learn and maintain and protect our ability to *speak from the heart*."
—John Bevere (Teaching from Session 9)

9.   Below are three words that are synonymous with the word *pretense*. How would you describe these words? What are their antonyms (opposites):

Counterfeit _____

_____

_____

_____

_____

_____

antonym _____

Charade _____

_____

_____

_____

_____

_____

antonym _____

Deception _____

_____

_____

_____

_____

_____

antonym _____

10.   Would you describe your honoring of God and those on your level as *true respect* or out of routine or habit? Again, get quiet and ask the Lord to show you your heart. **Write down** what He reveals to you.

_____

_____

_____

_____

_____

_____

_____

_____

_____

_____

_____

_____

_____

_____

_____

_____

_____

FASCINATING FACT:
He made free use of Christian vocabulary. He talked about the blessing of the Almighty and the Christian confessions which would become the pillars of the new government. He assumed the earnestness of a man weighed down by historic responsibility. He handed out pious stories to the press, especially to the church papers. He showed his tattered Bible and declared that he drew the strength for his great work from it as scores of pious people welcomed him as a man sent from God. Indeed, *Adolf Hitler* was a master of outward religiosity—with no inward reality![3]

11.   People who learn to love God but only show love to others in pretense are lacking...?

    a.   the human characteristic of humility.
    b.   the fear of the Lord.
    c.   an understanding of God's omnipotence.
    d.   a deeper revelation of the dispensation of grace.

> *Truths to Treasure*
>
> "...Because this people draw near with their words and honor Me with their lip service, but they remove their hearts far from Me, and their reverence for Me consists of tradition learned by *rote*."
> —*Isaiah 29:13 NASB*

12. God's Word has many things to say about wisdom and the fear of the Lord. **Read** and **take to heart** these powerful principles from the book of Proverbs. What are the specific blessing(s) found in each verse that directly results from the fear of the Lord?

Proverbs 1:7
The fear of the Lord gives me _____
_____
_____

Proverbs 2:4-6
Seeking Wisdom gives me _____
_____
_____

Proverbs 14:26, 27
The fear of the Lord gives me _____
_____
_____

Proverbs 16:6
The fear of the Lord gives me _____
_____
_____

Proverbs 19:23
The fear of the Lord gives me _____
_____
_____
_____
_____

INSTANT Replay

"The *fear of the Lord* keeps us aware of the fact that God knows in detail every thought and intent, along with every word we speak. Even idle words we will give an account of on the Day of Judgment."
—John Bevere (Page 155)

Truths to Treasure

"Come, you children, listen to me; I will teach you *the fear of the Lord*. Who is the man who desires life, and loves many days, that he may see good? *Keep your tongue from evil, and your lips from speaking deceit.* Depart from evil and do good; seek peace and pursue it."
—Psalm 34:11-14 NKJV

13. Psalm 34:11-14 shows us that there is a clear connection between the fear of the Lord and watching our words.

   a. **Write out** and **take to heart** these words of warning found in...

   Luke 8:17 _____
   _____
   _____
   _____

   Hebrews 4:13 _____
   _____
   _____
   _____

Also
Check out
Romans
14:12

   Matthew 12:36,37 _____
   _____
   _____
   _____

   b. In light of these Scriptures, explain why the fear of the Lord should cause us to carefully watch our words.

   _____
   _____
   _____
   _____
   _____
   _____

What is *the fear of the Lord* like?

Have you ever been to Niagara Falls or the Grand Canyon? When you're close to the edge of the falls, enveloped by the thunder and spray of 6 million cubic feet of water bursting over the falls every minute, or when you stand at the rim of the canyon and a sense of dizzying awe overwhelms you as you step back from the edge of that vast expanse and bottomless gorge—that is somewhat akin to the "fear of God." It isn't an unhealthy fear, but *an overwhelming sense of God Himself*. A.W. Tozer defined it as "astonishing reverence." William Anderson, in his book *The Faith That Satisfies*, wrote, "I was really surprised to find more than 300 references in the Old Testament that speak of the fear of the Lord.... The fear of the Lord is *reverential trust* and *hatred of evil*, and there you have the whole thing."[4]

Here's to your health—your spiritual, physical, mental and emotional health. Most of us will agree that our minds could definitely use some reprogramming in the area of honoring those on our level and walking in love. Romans 12:2 NLT says, "Don't copy the *behavior* and *customs* of this world, but let God transform you into a new person by changing the way you think...." There is no better way to change the way you think than by reprogramming your mind with the truth of God's Word!

HERE'S THE CHALLENGE:

Step 1 – **Read** 1 Corinthians 13:4-8 in two of your favorite versions of the Bible.
(We've provided you with *The Amplified Bible's* powerful and very descriptive version as an option.)

Step 2 – **Select** the version that impacts and ministers to you the most.

Step 3 – **Read out loud** the version you have selected *three* times a day, for the next 30 days (preferably morning, noon and night). Personalize the passage: Say, "I walk in love. I am patient and kind. I am not envious or jealous...."

Step 4 – **Observe** in amazement what takes place in your interactions with others and with God.

Step 5 – **Write down** your experiences and anything the Lord reveals to you.

1 Corinthians 13:4-8 AMP

Love endures long and is patient and kind; love never is envious nor boils over with jealousy, is not boastful or vainglorious, does not display itself haughtily.

It is not conceited (arrogant and inflated with pride); it is not rude (unmannerly) and does not act unbecomingly. Love (God's love in us) does not insist on its own rights or its own way, for it is not self-seeking; it is not touchy or fretful or resentful; it takes no account of the evil done to it [it pays no attention to a suffered wrong].

It does not rejoice at injustice and unrighteousness, but rejoices when right and truth prevail.

Love bears up under anything and everything that comes, is ever ready to believe the best of every person, its hopes are fadeless under all circumstances, and it endures everything [without weakening].

Love never fails [never fades out or becomes obsolete or comes to an end]....

Journal *Your* Journey

Date Started: _____

_____

_____

_____

_____

_____

_____

_____

_____

_____

_____

_____

_____

_____

_____

_____

_____

Date Completed: _____

Hide in Your Heart

HONOR PRINCIPLE 9

Honoring those *on our level*, our fellowman, also carries a reward and is just as important as honoring those who are over us. Jesus said, "A new command I give you: Love one another. As I have loved you, so you must *love one another*. By this all men will know that you are my disciples, if you love one another" (John 13:34,35 NIV).

LESSONS *from* LEADERS

"The mainspring of Paul's service is **not** *love for men*, but *love for Jesus Christ*. If we are devoted to the cause of humanity, we shall soon be crushed and brokenhearted, for we shall often meet with more ingratitude from men than we would from a dog; but if our motive is love to God, no ingratitude can hinder us from serving our fellow men."

—*Oswald Chambers*[5]

TRUE LOVE

"Let everything you do be done in love (**true love** to God and man as inspired by God's love for us)."

—1 Corinthians 16:14 AMP

Of the three different levels of people we can honor, we probably have the most opportunity to honor those *on our level*. As hard as it may seem at times, God has given us the ability to love people the way He loves us. Romans 5:5 NKJV says "...the love of God has been poured out in our hearts by the Holy Spirit who was given to us." So God's love *is* in us—it starts out as a seed, like all the other fruits of His character, and it grows over time and through experience.

Think for a moment. When you plant a seed in soil, what do you do to help it grow? You regularly water it and give it sunlight. In the same way, the divine Seed of Almighty God containing His spiritual DNA is planted in the soil of our spirit the moment we repent of our sins and accept Christ into our hearts (see 1 John 3:9). In order for this Seed to grow, we must regularly water it with the Word and give it plenty of "Sonlight"—time spent in His presence. Over time and through experience, the character of Christ begins to grow—including the character of His **love**.

INSTANT Replay

"The love of God is in our heart. We must *cooperate* with the Holy Spirit to develop it."
—**John Bevere** (Page 160)

Joyce Meyer has been profoundly preaching God's Word for nearly 30 years. During that time, she has taught on numerous topics, but few are closer to her heart than the topic of walking in love. Check out this excerpt from her article titled "How to Recognize a Hypocrite."

Love is not just a word. It is an action. Anytime you or I *talk* about love, yet fail to *show* love in our actions, we are being hypocritical.

True love originates from God (see 1 John 4:7,8). It flows from Him to us, we receive it, and then we choose to allow it to flow through us to others. True Christians pursue a strong love walk— they see it as a priority. Once we receive His love and begin to love ourselves, we are able to express genuine love to others.

One of the ways our love is seen and measured is in how we treat people. It is very important to God. I believe that it is the most important thing next to our salvation. Our faith is of little value if our lives lack love in action (see James 2:14,17). How else is the world going to know that we have love unless we express it to them in our actions?

"...Aim to show kindness and seek to do good to one another and to everybody" (1 Thessalonians 5:15 AMP). When we love others, we are *loving God*. He is always proud of us and pleased when we do something good for somebody else out of a pure heart. It is our love in action that sets us apart as true children of God. As we get our minds off of what we want and what we need and choose to help others, we will be motivated by love—the more excellent way (see 1 Corinthians 12:31).[6]

There are three specific things we need to guard against in order to be able to walk in love with our peers. These antagonistic enemies are *comparison*, *competition* and *selfish ambition*. What do these words mean, and how do you think they hinder us from honoring others?

Comparison _____

_____

_____

_____

_____

_____

Competition _____

_____

_____

_____

_____

_____

Selfish Ambition _____

_____

_____

_____

_____

_____

To *genuinely* *love* someone is to *honor* them. **Write out** and **take to heart** the power principles in the following verses and see what God says concerning the importance of love.

1 Corinthians 13:1-3, 13 _____

_____

_____

_____

_____

_____

1 John 4:7,8 _____

_____

_____

_____

_____

_____

_____

Romans 13:8 _____

_____

_____

_____

_____

_____

LESSONS *from* LEADERS

"Love is a *fruit in season* at all times, and within the reach of *every* hand."
                        —Mother Teresa[7]

Prayer

Change my heart, oh God. Help me to be sincere and express my feelings to others in a kind, loving and truthful way. Forgive me for being a hypocrite at times. Help me not say things just to sound spiritual or to act like I care. Help me to recognize and reject every thought that comes against me to compare and compete with others or be led by selfish ambition.

Holy Spirit, please teach me and instill in me the fear of the Lord. Show me how to keep my tongue from evil and lips from speaking deceit. Place a guard over my mouth (see Psalm 141:3). Help me to be sincere and real but not harsh and rude.

Father, I don't want to worship You and praise You just out of a habit or routine I learned from the traditions of my church. I want to worship You and honor You from the depths of my heart. I love You, Lord, and I thank You for opening my eyes to these truths. In Jesus' name, Amen!

INSTANT Replay

"I hope by now it's coming into clear view: To honor is to *genuinely love.*
It takes both *holy fear* and *unconditional love* to walk in true honor."
—John Bevere (Page 152)

EXPRESS YOUR EXPERIENCE

Take a moment to close your eyes and sit quietly before the Lord. Thank Him for His love and forgiveness and His mercy that is new every morning. Let Him open your spiritual eyes to the hidden treasure of who He is. Now reflect on the session: What is the greatest truth you have learned? Which Scripture(s) impacted you most? **Write out** any other insights the Holy Spirit reveals to you.

_____

_____

_____

_____

_____

_____

_____

_____

_____

_____

(1) Quotes on *Fellowship* (www.dailychristianquote.com, retrieved 8/27/07). (2) See note 1, quotes on *Honesty and Integrity*, retrieved 8/24/07. (3) Illustrations on *Hypocrisy* (www.sermonillustrations. com, retrieved 8/24/07). (4) *Nelson's Annual Preacher's Sourcebook 2002 Edition*, Robert J. Morgan, Editor (Thomas Nelson, Inc.: Nashville, TN 2001) p. 114. (5) Oswald Chambers, *My Utmost for His Highest – Selections for the Year* (Barbour Publishing, Inc.: Uhrichsville, OH) p. 54. (6) "How to Recognize a Hypocrite," Joyce Meyer, *Life In The Word* magazine, March 2001, *Joyce Meyer Ministries*, Inc., Fenton, MO). (7) Quotes on *Love* (www.motivational-inspirational-corner.com/motivational_inspirational_quotes.html, retrieved 8/24/07).

Notes

"When we choose to be *parents*, we accept another human being as part of ourselves, and a large part of our emotional selves will stay with that person as long as we live. From that time on, there will be another person on this earth whose orbit around us will affect us as surely as the moon affects the tides, and affect us in some ways more deeply than anyone else can. Our children are extensions of ourselves.

–"Mr." Fred Rogers[1]

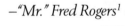

10 HONORING ENTRUSTED ONES PART 1

Please refer to Chapters 13 and 14 in the *Honor's Reward* book along with Session 10 of the teaching series.

NURTURE

To feed, to nourish; to educate, to bring up or train up.

— American Dictionary of the English Language, **Noah Webster 1828**

INSTANT *Replay*

"God is the One who delegates authority; He is love, and releases His authority for the purpose of *love* and *protection*. If it's instead used to abuse, take advantage of, or harm the little ones, it becomes a direct affront to *Him*."
—John Bevere (Page 162)

1. Who are the "little ones" the Scripture is referring to who have been entrusted to our authority?

    _____
    _____
    _____
    _____
    _____
    _____
    _____
    _____
    _____

> ### Truths to Treasure
>
> "It will be terrible for people who cause even one of my *little followers* to sin. Those people would be better off thrown into the deepest part of the ocean with a heavy stone tied around their necks! *Don't be cruel to any of these little ones!* I promise you that their angels are always with my Father in heaven."
> —*Matthew 18:6,10,11*
> *CEV*
> [Italics added for emphasis.]

2.   As someone in authority, what are some of your responsibilities
      to those who have been entrusted to you?

      _____

      _____

      _____

      _____

      _____

3.   Name the two extreme abuses of authority that cause little
      ones to stumble. As people in authority, how can we protect
      ourselves from these extremes?

      _____

      _____

      _____

      _____

      _____

      _____

      _____

4.   Some leaders accomplish a lot
      outwardly but leave bruised and
      wounded followers in their wake.
      On the other hand, there are
      leaders who accomplish much but
      also build others up in the process.

      a. What characteristic about a
          leader makes all the difference
          in the world?

          _____

          _____

          _____

          _____

      b. The *dishonoring* leader is *life-
          damaging*. How does he see
          the people entrusted to him?

          _____

          _____

          _____

          _____

Truths to Treasure

"I warn and counsel the elders among you (the pastors and spiritual guides of the church) as a fellow elder.... Tend (**nurture**, guard, guide, and fold) the flock of God that is [your responsibility], not by coercion or constraint, but willingly; not dishonorably motivated by the advantages and profits [belonging to the office], but eagerly and cheerfully; not domineering [as arrogant, dictatorial, and overbearing persons] over those in your charge, but being examples (patterns and models of Christian living) to the flock (the congregation)."

—1 Peter 5:1-3 AMP

c. The *honoring* leader is *life-enhancing*. How does he see the people entrusted to him?

_____

_____

_____

_____

d. As a parent, teacher, employer or church leader, are you more of an honoring leader or a dishonoring leader? In what areas can you improve?

_____

_____

_____

_____

LESSONS from LEADERS

"We must feel toward our people as a father toward his children; yea, the most *tender love* of a mother must not surpass ours. ...When the people see that you truly love them, they will hear anything from you.... Oh therefore, see that you feel a tender love for your people in your hearts, and *let them perceive it in your speech and conduct.* Let them see that you spend and are spent for their sakes."

–*Richard Baxter*[2]

---

5. An *honoring* leader will encourage the development of his people. What are the *two* greatest joys he desires those entrusted to him to experience? The combination of these two major aspects of the Christian life describes what?

_____

_____

_____

_____

_____

6. What does the wise, honoring leader continually do to those who serve under him?

_____

_____

_____

_____

_____

INSTANT *Replay*

"When the leader honors the little ones, it in turn releases
the gift of God in their lives. As their gift flourishes the leader
in turn benefits as his or her vision is accomplished through
all the gifts of the people combined in the organization."
—John Bevere (Pages 170-171)

CORRECTION

The act of bringing back, from error or deviation, to a just standard, as to truth,
rectitude [righteousness], justice or propriety [respectability].

– American Dictionary of the English Language, **Noah Webster 1828**
[Words in brackets added for clarity].

---

7.   How do you feel when someone brings correction to you using
shame, condemnation or *guilt*? How do you feel when God
corrects you? Can you recognize the difference? What is it?

_____

_____

_____

_____

_____

LESSONS *from* LEADERS

"Spare the rod and spoil the child—that is true. But, beside the rod, keep an apple to
give him when he has done well."

—Martin Luther[3]

8.   Holding a grudge against someone under your authority is very
damaging. It affects you and all your relationships. It can also
hinder your prayers and even separate you from the Father.

**Also
Check out**
Matthew
6:14,15

a.   **Write out** and **take to heart** Jesus' warning in Mark 11:25,
26 about holding on to the mistakes of others.

_____

_____

_____

b. **Write out** and **take to heart** Psalm 103:12, declaring what God does with our mistakes when we ask Him to forgive us.

_____

_____

_____

INSTANT *Replay*

"True fathers and mothers [both in the home and in the church] desire their children to *surpass* their own success. Jesus stated His desire for us: to do greater works than He did. We should have the same heart for those who follow us."

—John Bevere (Page 168)
[Words in brackets added
for clarification and emphasis.]

Truths to Treasure

"Fathers, do not irritate and provoke your children to anger [do not exasperate them to resentment], but rear them [tenderly] in the training and discipline and the counsel and admonition of the Lord."
—Ephesians 6:4 AMP

9. When correcting our children or anyone else under our authority, we must

    a. be careful not to attack their character but instead deal with their behavior.
    b. do it in front of others so that everyone can see the consequences of wrong behavior.
    c. always smile and laugh and never raise our voice.
    d. repeat to them all that they did wrong in a strong enough way that they feel badly about what they did.

10. It is evident from Scripture that as admirable as David was in some areas, he failed to discipline his children—specifically Amnon and Absalom. As a result, their lives and the lives of those around them experienced great tragedy. **Write out** what each of these Scriptures mean to you personally concerning the discipline of your children.

    Proverbs 13:24 _____

    _____

    _____

    _____

    _____

    _____

    _____

Proverbs 22:6, 15 _____

_____

_____

_____

_____

_____

_____

Proverbs 29:15 _____

_____

_____

_____

_____

_____

_____

LESSONS from LEADERS

"...When the child, aged two to ten, fully understands what he is being asked to do but refuses to yield to adult leadership, an appropriate spanking is the shortest and most effective route to an attitude adjustment. ...Children who have experienced corporal punishment from *loving parents* do not have trouble understanding its meaning. ...A boy or girl who knows that love abounds at home will not resent a well-deserved spanking. One who is *unloved* or *ignored* will hate any form of discipline!"

–Dr. James Dobson[4]

---

11.   **Meditate on the message** of the three Scriptures from Proverbs. Get quiet and ask the Holy Spirit to show you how your discipline lines up with them. **Write out** any insights He reveals to you.

_____

_____

_____

_____

12.   Do you know a family member or friend who refrained from using the rod and restrictions when disciplining their children and instead tried to "love" them into right behavior? What was the result of their parenting?

_____

_____

_____

_____

13. As a youth pastor, John discovered a pattern in the parent-child relationship in regard to correction that is worth remembering. **Write out** the two common trends he observed.

_____

_____

_____

_____

INSTANT Replay

"After seven years of serving in a local church and almost twenty years of traveling ministry, I've observed the *greatest need for honor* isn't in the church or the workplace, but rather *in our homes*. The truth is, social, civil and church arenas would all greatly benefit if fathers and mothers exemplified honor in their homes...."
—John Bevere (Page 175)

DIG Deeper

As a parent, employer, church leader, etc., it is very important for us to *think highly* of those who are under our authority. We will all go through times when all we seem to see are the negative traits and immaturity of those entrusted to us. However, we need to guard ourselves from constantly focusing on their flaws. By guarding our hearts and choosing to think highly of them, we can maintain an ample supply of true honor for them in our hearts.

Is there someone under your authority whom you are having a difficult time honoring? Maybe it is one of your children, an employee or someone in ministry under you who has a bad attitude or is behaving poorly. Take a few minutes and read Philippians 4:8 again. Read it out loud and meditate on its message. Now write the name of the person entrusted to you whom

Ponder the Principle

"For the rest, brethren, whatever is *true*, whatever is worthy of reverence and is *honorable* and *seemly*, whatever is *just*, whatever is *pure*, whatever is *lovely* and *lovable*, whatever is *kind* and *winsome* and *gracious*, if there is any *virtue* and *excellence*, if there is anything *worthy of praise*, think on and weigh and take account of these things **[fix your minds on them]**."

—Philippians 4:8 AMP
[Italics and bold added for emphasis.]

you are having difficulty with and **write out** as many of the positive qualities you can think of that they possess.

The person I am struggling to honor in my heart is

_____.

Yet, I _choose_ to focus on and thank God for their _positive_ qualities including...

_____
_____
_____
_____
_____
_____

Journal Your Journey

After you've done the above exercise for a couple of weeks, **write down** what happens in your heart, as well as any notable changes in your relationship with the person.

_____
_____
_____
_____
_____
_____
_____
_____
_____
_____

This exercise can and should be applied to any person _under_ you, _over_ you or _on your level_ whom you are having difficulty honoring. Focusing on a person's positive qualities and thanking God for them is a powerful weapon against the enemy of offense that so often tries to bring strife to separate us from those we love.

Hide in Your Heart

HONOR PRINCIPLE 10

"And whoever [honors] one of these _little ones_ [with] only a cup of cold water in the name of a disciple, assuredly, I say to you, he shall by no means lose his _reward_" (Matthew 10:42 NKJV). In the Scripture, "little ones" are identified as small children or those entrusted to our delegated authority.

[Words in brackets added for clarity and emphasis.]

CHILDREN ARE TREASURES!

"Don't you see that *children are God's best gift?* The fruit of the womb his generous legacy? Like a warrior's fistful of arrows are the children of a vigorous youth. Oh, how blessed are you parents, with your quivers full of children!"

—Psalm 127:3,4 The Message

Remember the old saying, "Sticks and stones can break my bones, but *words* can never hurt me"? Few things could be further from the truth. The reality is, sticks and stones may cause physical pain, but some of life's deepest wounds result from the words spoken to us— especially by our parents. Undoubtedly, a parent's words carry great weight in a child's life.

As John mentioned, one of the worst ways we as parents can dishonor our children is by *ignoring* them. In many cases, this ac- tually does more damage to their development than harsh words. TV legend and children's advocate Bob Keeshan, better known for his 36-year role as Captain Kangaroo,[5] had some striking things to say on the importance of talking to and spending time with our children:

"A small child waits with impatience the arrival home of a parent. She wishes to relate some sandbox experience. She is excited to share the thrill that she has known that day. The time comes; the parent arrives. Beaten down by the stresses of the workplace, the parent often replies: 'Not now, honey, I'm busy. Go watch tele- vision.'

The most often spoken words in the American household today are the words: go watch television. If not now, when? Later. But later never comes for many, and the parent fails to communicate at the very earliest of ages. We give her designer clothes and computer toys, but we do not give her what she wants the most, which is our *time.* Now she is fifteen and has a glassy look in her eyes. 'Honey, do we need to sit down and talk?' Too late. Love has passed by."[6]

Clearly, communicating with our kids is crucial to their well-being. What we say and how we say it is equally important. Our words are containers of power, continuously shaping the souls of our little ones. It may seem like they will be with us forever, but the time we have with them is brief in comparison to the overall big picture.

LESSONS from LEADERS

"Affirming words from moms and dads are like *light switches.* Speak a word of affirmation at the right moment in a child's life and it's like lighting up a whole roomful of possibilities."

–*Gary Smalley*[7]

Take a few minutes to carefully and prayerfully answer these soul-searching questions.

Do you feel in your heart that you give your children the time and attention they need? What is the greatest obstacle(s) to you spending time with them? Surrender it to God and ask Him to help you prioritize your responsibilities and invest your time wisely.

_____

_____

_____

_____

_____

_____

_____

_____

Write out some of the specific words and phrases that come out of your mouth on a regular basis when talking with your children. Are they *negative* words that tear down or *positive* words that build up? Ask God to give you some better word choices for the ones that need replacing. Write them out, and by God's grace, begin putting them into practice.

Ponder the Principle

"Look *carefully* then how you walk! Live *purposefully* and worthily and accurately, not as the unwise and witless, but as wise (sensible, intelligent people), *making the very most of the time* [buying up each opportunity], because the days are evil. Therefore do not be vague and thoughtless and foolish, but understanding and firmly grasping what the will of the Lord is."

–*Ephesians 5:15-17 AMP*

_____

_____

_____

_____

_____

> **FASCINATING FACT:**
> A survey asked mothers to keep track of how many times they made negative, compared with positive, comments to their children. They admitted that they criticized ten times for every time they said something favorable. A three-year survey in one city's schools found that the teachers were 75 percent negative. The study indicated that it takes *four positive statements* from a teacher to offset the effects of *one negative statement* to a child.[8]

Our sons and daughters desperately desire to be approved of by us. Therefore, when we as parents give correction, we must be careful not to always focus or harp on their immature traits and weaknesses. This can often lead to them becoming exactly what we are trying to help them avoid.

Read Romans 4:17, which describes one of the ways God uses His words. Then read and meditate on the principles of Proverbs 18:21 and Ephesians 5:1. **Write out** the overall instruction you receive concerning the way you should speak *to* and *about* your children.

_____
_____
_____
_____
_____
_____
_____
_____
_____
_____
_____
_____
_____
_____
_____
_____
_____
_____

INSTANT *Replay*

"Children require frequent encouragement, direction, and affirmation.
They need to be *told*, as well as *shown*, they are loved and valued.
If not, chances are good they'll seek it in the wrong places."
—John Bevere (Page 178)

There is a lot of power in a person's name. From the day someone is born until the day they leave this life, a person is constantly being called by their name, and consequently, they are being called what their name means. Using a baby name book or an online search, **write out** the names of each of your children and their meanings (first and middle names). Then do the same with your name.

_____ -	_____
Child's name (first and then middle)	The meaning of their name (first and then middle)
_____ -	_____
Child's name (first and then middle)	The meaning of their name (first and then middle)
_____ -	_____
Child's name (first and then middle)	The meaning of their name (first and then middle)
_____ -	_____
Your name (first and then middle)	The meaning of your name (first and then middle)

Note: Every time you call your child's name, you are declaring that they are what their name means.

Go the Extra Mile!
Get a Bible concordance and find a few key Scriptures that support and reinforce the positive qualities attached to your child's name. Write them out and begin to proclaim them daily, out loud, over your child in your prayer time. As you are diligent to declare God's Word over your children, you will be amazed at the transformation it brings!

Prayer of Forgiveness

Father, please forgive me for neglecting or ignoring my children at times and for every harsh word I have carelessly spoken to them. Heal the wounds in their souls I may have caused and help me to reprogram my mind and mouth with the right things (see Philippians 4:8).

You know the hurtful things that were spoken to me as a child. Please heal my inner wounds and remove every harsh word from my vocabulary. Help me to begin focusing my thoughts on the positive traits of my children and declare Your Word over their lives according to Romans 4:17.

I love You, Lord, and I thank You for working in my life. In Jesus' name, Amen!

EXPRESS YOUR EXPERIENCE

Romans 8:1 NIV declares that there is "...no condemnation for those who are in Christ Jesus." If you have fallen short in the way you've treated those under your authority, don't feel condemned. Ask God to forgive you, receive His love, and let Him work through you to honor those He has entrusted to your care.

Take a few minutes and write down what impacted you the most from this week's session. Which Scripture(s) really struck a cord? In what ways are you challenged to come up higher? Write down anything the Holy Spirit reveals or asks you to do.

_____
_____
_____
_____
_____
_____
_____
_____
_____
_____
_____
_____
_____
_____
_____
_____
_____
_____
_____
_____
_____
_____
_____
_____
_____

Please Note: the next chapter is written for husbands only.

(1) Parenting Quotes and Parent Quotes (www.great-inspirational-quotes.com/parenting-quotes. html, retrieved 8/13/07). (2) Quotes on Leadership and Pastoral (www.dailychristianquote.com, retrieved 9/12/07). (3) Quotes on Children and Family, see note 2. (4) Dr. James Dobson, *Solid Answers* (Tyndale House Publishing: Wheaton, IL, 1997) p.137-139. (5) *TV's 'Captain Kangaroo,' Bob Keeshan, Dead* (www.cnn.com/2004/SHOWBIZ/TV/01/23/obit.kangaroo/, retrieved 9/12/07). (6) Illustrations on *Father* (www.sermonillustrations.com, retrieved 8/10/07). (7) See note 1, retrieved 8/11/07. (8) Illustrations on Criticism (www.sermonillustrations.com, retrieved 7/25/07).

"A man doesn't *own* his marriage; he is only the *steward* of his wife's love."

–*Ed Cole*[1]

11

HONORING
ENTRUSTED ONES PART 2

Please refer to Chapter 15 in the *Honor's Reward* book along with Session 11 of the teaching series. (Women may skip this chapter.)

MARRIAGE

The rendering of several words and phrases in the Hebrew and Greek, meaning to be "master"; to "take," that is, a wife; to "magnify" or "lift up" a woman; to "contract"; to "dwell together"; to "perform the duty of a brother"; to "become," that is, the wife of one. In all the Hebrew Scriptures there is no single word for the state of marriage to express the abstract idea of wedlock.[2]

1. Proverbs 18:22 CEV says, "A man's *greatest treasure* is his wife—she is a *gift* from the Lord." Husbands, how are you treating God's gift to you? How are you showing her that she is *valuable, precious* and *worthy of respect* and *esteem*?

   _____
   _____
   _____
   _____
   _____
   _____
   _____
   _____
   _____
   _____
   _____
   _____

> ### Hide in Your Heart
>
> **HONOR PRINCIPLE 11**
> "...Husbands must *give honor* to your wives. Treat your wife with understanding as you live together. She may be weaker than you are, but she is your *equal* partner in God's gift of new life. Treat her as you should so your prayers will not be hindered."
>
> *—1 Peter 3:7 NLT*

2. In 1 Peter 3:7 we learn that we are to honor our wives in two ways: as the *weaker vessel* and a *joint heir* in the grace of life.

   a. List at least *five* or more practical ways you can give your wife honor.

   _____

   _____

   _____

   _____

   _____

   b. What does it mean to be a *joint heir* in the grace of life?

   _____

   _____

   _____

   _____

   _____

INSTANT Replay

"Some men interpret [1 Peter 3:7] as the wife being beneath her husband in spiritual things. No. 'Weaker vessel' *doesn't mean your wife is below you*; it only means she can't bench-press as much as you. The physical strength of the average woman is less than the average man."
—John Bevere (Page 187)
[Words in brackets added for clarification.]

3. When it comes to making decisions, especially those that affect the family, do you consult your wife and ask for her input?

   _____

   a. Why or why not?

   _____

   _____

   _____

   b. What did the Lord show John that a *wise* leader must learn to do in order to be able to make Spirit-led decisions?

   _____

   _____

   _____

4. How do you view your wife's level of spiritual maturity? (This includes things like her prayer life, knowledge of the Word and overall intimacy with God.) In your prayer time, ask God to help you see your wife's spiritual maturity the way *He* sees it, and write down what He reveals to you.

    _____

    _____

    _____

    _____

    _____

    _____

LESSONS from LEADERS

"Eve was *not* taken out of Adam's head to top him, neither out of his feet to be trampled on by him, but out of his side to be *equal* with him, under his arm to be protected by him, and near his heart to be *loved* by him."

–*Matthew Henry*[3]

5. In Genesis 1:27, we discover something very important about the full, complete image of God. What is it? **Write out** and **take to heart** the related principle found in 1 Corinthians 11:11.

    _____

    _____

    _____

    _____

    _____

    _____

    _____

    _____

> ### Truths to Treasure
>
> "So God created man [mankind, human beings] in His own image; in the image of God He created him; *male and female* He created them."
>
> –*Genesis 1:27 NKJV*
> *[Words in brackets added for clarity and emphasis.]*

6. Men, our wives deserve honor. They should be treated as *equal*, not less than or lower than us. What is the catastrophic consequence of failing to honor our wives? Does this speak anything to you specifically?

    _____

    _____

    _____

    _____

    _____

LESSONS from LEADERS

"Part of dwelling with your wife *with understanding* means recognizing that your wife is in need of your *covering, protection,* and *love.* And because you are *heirs together* of God's grace, you need to *honor* her in your **thoughts, words,** and **actions.** When you don't, your *prayers are hindered.* This means *all* of your prayers, not just those for your wife."

—Stormie Omartian[4]

7. The apostle Paul addresses the relationship between husbands and wives in several places in the New Testament. **Read** and **meditate on the message** of Ephesians 5:25-27.

> *Truths to Treasure*
>
> "Husbands, *go all out* in your love for your wives, exactly *as Christ did* for the church—a love marked by *giving,* not getting."
>
> *—Ephesians 5:25*
> *The Message*

   a. In verse 25, who is "the church"?

   _____

   _____

   _____

   _____

   _____

   _____

Check out
Hebrews
10:10,14;
1 Peter 2:24;
John 6:51

   b. What did Jesus do *specifically* for the church?

   _____

   _____

   _____

   _____

   c. What do you think it means for husbands to love their wives "as Christ loved the church"?

   _____

   _____

   _____

   _____

   d. **Write out** and **take to heart** the related power principle in Colossians 3:19.

   _____

   _____

   _____

   _____

8. **Read** Ephesians 5:28,29,33. All three of these verses talk about husbands loving their wives *as they love their own bodies*, nourishing and cherishing them.

    a. What does this mean, or say, to you?

    _____

    _____

    _____

    _____

    b. In what ways do we nourish and cherish our bodies? What do we *not* do to our bodies?

    _____

    _____

    _____

    _____

INSTANT Replay

"There is so much more understanding to be gained from the Word of God on how to dwell successfully in marriage with your wife. Many divorces could be averted if men only took the time to seek the wisdom of how women differ from men."
—**John Bevere** (Page 190)

LESSONS from LEADERS

"Where does your marriage rank on your hierarchy of values? Does it get the leftovers and scraps from your busy schedule, or is it something of great worth to be preserved and supported? It can die if left untended."

–*Dr. James Dobson*[5]

9. John shares how his wife, Lisa, lost her right eye to cancer at age five and has had to wear a prosthesis since then. As a result, she experienced a lot of ridicule and rejection while growing up. However, by God's grace and John's encouragement, she faced her fears head on and overcame them.

    a. What is one of your wife's greatest fears? When did it begin in her life and what was the cause? If you don't know, make a point to ask her.

    _____

    _____

    _____

    _____

    _____

b. In what ways can you encourage her and help her overcome her fears?

_____

_____

_____

_____

_____

_____

c. Get a Bible concordance and **write out** a few Scriptures that proclaim victory over the *specific* fear she is battling. For example, if your wife battles a fear of not knowing what to say when she gets in front of people, speak Luke 12:12 out loud over her, which declares that the Holy Spirit will teach her what to say.

_____

_____

_____

_____

_____

_____

10. As John encouraged Lisa and helped her overcome her fears, the Lord helped her discover and develop her gifts and talents. She is now flourishing more fully in her God-given calling.

a. Do you know the calling of God on your wife's life? Have you ever talked with her about it? If so, what has she shared with you?

_____

_____

_____

_____

_____

_____

> *Truths to Treasure*
>
> "Each person is given *something to do* that shows who God is: Everyone gets in on it, everyone benefits. All kinds of things are handed out by the Spirit, and to all kinds of people! The variety is wonderful...."
>
> *—1 Corinthians 12:7,8*
> *The Message*

b. Our life calling is defined to a great degree by our natural gifts and talents, as well as the things we enjoy doing. What kind of things is your wife gifted in? What does she enjoy doing? What is she passionate about?

_____

_____

_____

_____

_____

11. When we get sick, we often go to the doctor to find out what's wrong with us. Along with his examination, he asks us to describe the *symptoms* we are dealing with in order to properly diagnose what we have.

> ## LESSONS *from* LEADERS
>
> "Each one of us has a *fire* in our heart for something. It's our goal in life to find it and *keep it lit.*"
> —*Mary Lou Retton*[6]

a. What are the negative symptoms of *not* living in the call of God on your life?

_____

_____

_____

b. What are the *positive* results of living in the call of God on your life?

_____

_____

_____

_____

c. Which one would you say best describes your wife's condition? Why?

_____

_____

_____

_____

d. In what ways have you personally benefited from honoring your wife and helping her fulfill the call on her life?

_____

_____

_____

_____

INSTANT *Replay*

"We don't honor just to get a reward; we honor because it is the heart of God and it is our delight. Rewards follow all true honor. So husbands, don't delay. Honor your wife as a way of life; the reward God has to give to you through her is more than you can imagine."
—John Bevere (Page 200)

One of the best ways to honor your wife is to become a student of her life. Being a student means studying your "subject" closely and knowing all you can about her. Here are some practical, thought-provoking questions to help you get started. To make your fact-gathering time more fun-filled, why not plan a picnic lunch in the park for two or a candlelight dinner at a local restaurant.

THESE ARE A FEW OF HER FAVORITE THINGS

My wife's **name** is _____. Her name means
_____.

My wife's favorite **color** is _____.

My wife's favorite **flower** is _____.

My wife's favorite **food** is _____, and her favorite **restaurant** is _____.

My wife's favorite **movie** is _____, and her favorite kind of **music** is _____.

My wife's favorite **childhood memory** is _____
_____
_____.

My wife's favorite **pastime/hobby** is _____.

My wife's favorite **Bible character or Scripture** is _____
_____ because _____
_____.

My wife's *other* favorites are _____

_____

_____

_____

_____

_____.

**HEAR HER HEARTBEAT ON HOW SHE
FEELS ABOUT LIFE**

What makes her feel *safe* and *secure*?

_____

_____

_____

> ## LESSONS *from* LEADERS
> "The word *romance*, according to the dictionary, means 'excitement, adventure, and something extremely real.' Romance should last a *lifetime*."
> —*Billy Graham*[7]

What makes her feel *afraid* and *insecure*?

_____

_____

_____

What makes her feel *needed*?

_____

_____

_____

What makes her feel *loved* and *appreciated*?

_____

_____

_____

What makes her feel *peaceful* and *relaxed*?

_____

_____

_____

What things does she *like most* about herself?

_____

_____

_____

_____

What things does she *like least* about herself?

_____
_____
_____
_____

What are some of her *short-term* goals?

_____
_____
_____

What are some of her *long-term* goals?

_____
_____
_____

Remember, be sincere and write down what she says. You may be surprised by some of her answers.

INFO TO GO

Put some *legs* to your love!

Here are some romantic ideas to help you honor your wife and hit a home run in her heart.

- Fix her favorite breakfast and serve it to her in bed. Wake her up with a kiss, and sit in a chair by the bed and talk with her while she eats.

- Buy a pad of sticky notes and write a special message of love and appreciation on each. Hide them in different places where she is sure to find them.

- In front of a gathering of people—perhaps at a family reunion or holiday get-together—praise your wife, genuinely saying how much you love, appreciate and value her (be specific).

- Do a project around the house that she has requested but has been on the "back burner."

- One Saturday morning, tell her she's "Queen for the Day." Handle all her household responsibilities—cleaning, cooking, taking care of the kids, etc. Let her spend the day as she chooses.

LEAVE ROOM FOR THE LADIES

"'In the last days,' God says, 'I will pour out my Spirit upon all people. Your sons and *daughters* will prophesy. Your young men will see visions, and your old men will dream dreams. In those days I will pour out my Spirit even on my servants–men and *women* alike–and they will prophesy.'"

–Acts 2:17,18 NLT

If there is any one topic that has been a source of controversy in Christian circles down through the centuries, it is the role of women in ministry. Different individuals and denominations have different opinions on the issue. But there is one thing very evident in Scripture–God used women at key times and in key places to both preserve and advance His kingdom.

God used **Sarah** to give birth to Isaac, the child of promise, and Moses' sister, **Miriam**, as a prophetess to help lead Israel. He used **Rahab**, who had great faith, to protect the two Israelite spies from the leaders of Jericho, and He positioned **Ruth** to become David's great-grandmother.

Then there was **Deborah**, who served the Lord as both a prophetess and a judge over Israel; and **Hannah**, the faith-filled female who gave birth to the prophet Samuel. Of course we can't omit **Esther**, the Jewish girl God raised up to save her people from annihilation at the hands of Haman.

The list goes on and on, crossing the boundaries of time and testament to God's selection of **Mary**, whose bittersweet life gave birth to the Savior of the world; and **Anna**, the faithful prophetess, who was one of the earliest evangelists to proclaim the arrival of Jesus to the Jews.

Years ago, Dr. Yonggi Cho, senior pastor of Yoido Full Gospel Church–the world's largest church located in Seoul, Korea, with over 760,000 members–talked with Loren Cunningham, cofounder of the global ministry *Youth With A Mission (YWAM)*. The topic of their discussion was women in ministry. Here's an interesting excerpt of their conversation as told by Loren:

> *Ponder the Principle*
>
> "The Lord gives the word [of power]; the *women* who bear and publish [the news] are a great host."
> *–Psalm 68:11 AMP*

"...I saw Dr. Cho at a large event in the Olympic Stadium in Berlin where we were both speaking. He told me about a country he had just visited where the work of God had struggled for many years.

'All their churches are so little!' he said. 'And all of them are holding back their women, not allowing them to do what God calls them to do. They ask me, 'What's the key to your church?' I tell them again, 'Release your women,' but they just don't hear me!'

How sad that these leaders won't follow the example of the world's most successful pastor. Dr. Cho has 700 senior pastors on his staff, including many women. He also has 30,000 cell groups; the vast majority of these are led by women. Do you think God might be trying to tell all of us something?

...I want to champion the right of women and men to choose the call of God in their lives and to give more and more people the opportunity to serve the body of Christ with their gifts. Some women are called to be leaders; some are called to be homemakers. Women must have the freedom to obey God and be fulfilled in the gifts He has given them.

...My passion comes from four decades of ministry, leading cross-cultural mission efforts in every country on earth. My heart's desire is to see the mightiest missionary workforce in history unleashed. As we release women, we'll mobilize the hundreds of thousands of people needed to complete the Great Commission."[8]

God chooses who He wants to minister His Word, and He gives them— men and women alike—the grace they need to fulfill that call. There is no denying that God chose women like Kathryn Kuhlman, Aimee Semple McPherson and Joyce Meyer to minister His Word to the multitudes. How can we tell? The proof is in the fruit of changed lives.

INSTANT Replay

"How can we fulfill the Great Commission if over half the body of Christ is not honored to fulfill their calling? When men nurture the call of God in their wives' lives, they will receive a great reward. I've seen this in my own life."
—John Bevere (Page 194)

What powerful perspective has John discovered about families and churches that view women as spiritually inferior to men?

_____

_____

_____

_____

Read Luke 24:1,9,10. Who were the faithful few to arrive first at the tomb after Jesus rose from the grave?

_____

_____

_____

_____

Who was the *first* person to actually see Jesus after He had risen from the grave? What significant assignment did Jesus give to this person? What would we call this person today?

Check out John 20:10-18

_____

_____

_____

_____

How do you personally feel about women being in ministry as church leaders? How is your perspective different now than before this week's session? What changed it?

_____

_____

_____

_____

_____

_____

_____

_____

Whether it's the ministry of motherhood, the way Hannah and Mary served, the ministry of civil authority where Deborah and Esther served, or the ministry of preaching and prophesying, like Mary Magdalene and Miriam did respectively, women have played an important part in all that God is doing, and they continue to do so.

Is this to say that God prefers women over men? No. He is an *equal* opportunity anointer who wishes to pour out His Spirit on ALL flesh—men and women alike. So men, let's leave room for the ladies and not limit them in what they can do. As everyone does their part, we will make a difference!

Prayer for Men

Lord, thank You for opening my eyes to the truths of this session. I ask You to forgive me for any chauvinistic thinking that has clouded and distorted my thoughts, words and actions. Help me to support and encourage my wife in the call You have on her life. May I cover her with Your Word in prayer and help her uncover her gifts and talents.

I want to be the husband that my wife needs, but I can only do it in Your strength. Lord, give me the wisdom, creativity and motivation I need to honor and genuinely love her for our lifetime. She is Your gift to me, and I don't want to take her for granted.

Heal us both from the hurts we've caused each other. And bless our relationship with a fresh fire of desire for each other to be best friends and partners in life. In Jesus' name, Amen!

EXPRESS YOUR EXPERIENCE

Take a few moments to meditate on this week's session. What part impacted you the most? In what ways has your thinking been challenged to change? Is there anything that the Holy Spirit is asking you to do differently in regard to honoring your wife?

_____

_____

_____

_____

_____

_____

_____

_____

_____

_____

_____

_____

_____

_____

(1) Ed Cole Library, *Coleisms* (www.edcole.org/coleism, retrieved 9/18/07). (2) *The New Unger's Bible Dictionary*, Merrill F. Unger, R.K. Harrison, Editor (Chicago, IL: Moody Press, 1988) p.817. (3) Quotes on *Marriage* (www.dailychristianquote.com, retrieved 8/10/07). (4) Stormie Omartian, *The Power of a Praying Husband* (Harvest House Publishers, Eugene OR 2001) p. 33. (5) Dr. James Dobson, *Solid Answers* (Tyndale House Publishing: Wheaton, IL, 1997) p.544. (6) Quotes on *purpose*, retrieved 6/6/07 (www.motivational-inspirational-corner.com). (7) Quotes by *Clergymen* (www.brainyquote.com/quotes/type/type_clergyman.html, retrieved 9/18/07). (8) *Women in Leadership*, Loren Cunningham, *Enjoying Everyday Life* magazine, April 2006, Joyce Meyer Ministries, Inc., Fenton, MO) pp. 15,16.

Notes

"We do not segment our lives, giving some time to God, some to our business or schooling, while keeping parts to ourselves. The idea is *to live all of our lives* in the presence of God, under the authority of God, and for the *honor* and *glory* of **God**. That is what the Christian life is all about."

–R. C. *Sproul*[1]

12 HONORING GOD

Please refer to Chapters 16 and 17 in the *Honor's Reward* book along with Session 12 of the teaching series.

HONOR

"The rendering of several Hebrew and Greek words, meaning *respect* paid to superiors, such as to God, to parents and kings, including *submission* and *service*.[2] The word honor is primarily '**a valuing**.'[3]"

INSTANT Replay

"The only way to walk in true honor is to first and foremost *always honor* God. Enduring honor is found only in valuing Him above anything or anyone else."
—**John Bevere** (Page 209)

1. The ability to honor those over us, on our level and entrusted to our care is birthed out of a heart of honor for God. To Him alone does our honor transcend into worship. **Write out** and **take to heart** God's *grand command* found in Mark 12:30.

_____

_____

_____

_____

_____

_____

_____

_____

_____

2. Eli the priest dishonored God *greatly* because he...

   a. lacked spiritual discernment and failed to bring the word of the Lord to the people.

   b. was a glutton and ate too much of the meat offerings brought to the temple.

   c. responded rudely to Hannah and was insensitive to her as she prayed for a child.

   d. honored his sons more than God and failed to remove them from their positions of authority for their deplorable behavior.

3. Have you ever honored (valued, esteemed, respected) your spouse, children or friend *more than* God? Explain the situation and the "fruit" it produced.

_____

_____

_____

_____

_____

INSTANT *Replay*

"When we compromise the will of God, as revealed in His Word,
in order to honor someone, even if it's within our own family,
we in essence sin against God."
—John Bevere (Page 216)

4. Eli was *judged* for dishonoring God, and Abraham was *blessed* for honoring God. What were the consequences of their actions, and who felt the effects?

Eli's Consequences
(See 1 Samuel 2:27-36.)

_____

_____

_____

_____

_____

_____

> ### Truths to Treasure
>
> "He who loves [honors] father or mother more than Me is not worthy of Me; and he who loves [honors] son or daughter more than Me is not worthy of Me."
>
> *—Matthew 10:37 NASB*
> *[Words in brackets added for emphasis.]*

Abraham's Blessings (See Genesis 22:15-18.)

_____

_____

_____

_____

5. Abraham's actions toward God were quite different than Eli's. When God asked him to sacrifice the greatest thing he had—his son—he promptly responded in obedience.

    a. Abraham's quick response indicates a heart of honor founded on what? (See Genesis 22:12.)

    _____

    _____

    _____

    _____

    _____

    b. When God asks you to do something, how quickly do you respond?

    _____

    _____

    _____

    _____

    _____

6. In the story about Moses and his wife, Zipporah, Moses chose to honor his wife's demands over God's commands. He became frustrated with Zipporah's resistance and gave in to her to keep the peace between them.

    a. What is the difference between being a *peacekeeper* and being a *peacemaker*?

    _____

    _____

    _____

    _____

    _____

    _____

    _____

Truths to Treasure

"...Eye has not seen and ear has not heard and has not entered into the heart of man, [all that] God has prepared (made and keeps ready) for those who love Him [who hold Him in affectionate reverence, **promptly obeying Him** and gratefully recognizing the benefits He has bestowed]."
—1 Corinthians 2:9 AMP

**Check out
& write out**
Matthew 5:9

b. Which one has God's blessing?

_____

_____

_____

7. According to God's order of authority, husbands are the head of the home (see Ephesians 5:23). This makes them ultimately *accountable* to God for the overall supervision of the family. Just as God gave direction to Moses, He gives husbands and fathers direction for their families.

   a. Men, what does Moses' situation with Zipporah say to you about following through with what God speaks to you?

_____

_____

_____

   b. Ladies, what does the situation say to you about submitting to your husband's leadership?

_____

_____

_____

8. When Peter and some of the other disciples were preaching the good news of Jesus after His resurrection, the church leaders told them to stop. How did Peter respond? What does this example say to you?

Check out
Acts 5:27-29

_____

_____

_____

_____

_____

_____

_____

_____

> **LESSONS** *from* **LEADERS**
>
> "It is only the *fear of God* that can deliver us from the *fear of man*."
> —*John Witherspoon*[4]

INSTANT Replay

"...Sometimes it's easier to honor the one we face than the One we cannot see. However, this must not be so. We must set boundaries of convictions in our lives to regulate our responses. So if someone we respect or love asks, entices, or tries to persuade us to go *against* what we know to be the Word of God, we *cannot honor their wishes above God's.*"

—John Bevere (Page 219)

9. According to Scripture, there are some rare occasions when we are to *withhold* honor. Proverbs 26:8 NLT declares, "Honoring a fool is as foolish as tying a stone to a slingshot." In other words, honoring a fool only brings harm to us.

a. What are some of the characteristics of a fool mentioned in Scripture?

Check out Psalm 53:1; Proverbs 10:18,23; 12:15; 14:3; 15:5; 18:2

_____

_____

_____

_____

_____

b. What name is often used in the New Testament to refer to a fool? Why?

_____

_____

_____

_____

_____

c. We are to honor a fool as a person and walk in love toward them, but we are not to honor a fool *for* their folly—behavior that goes against the truth of God's Word. If we honor (esteem, value) a fool for (or in) their folly, we become what? (See 2 John 10,11.)

_____

_____

_____

_____

_____

INSTANT Replay

"[The Samaritan] didn't need to hear a word from God, nor did he have to pray about it. Out of a heart of *love, compassion,* and *respect* for other individuals, he did what was necessary. This is a classic example of honoring all men."

—John Bevere (page 202)

[Words in brackets added for clarity.]

> ### Truths to Treasure
>
> "Honor *all people.* Love the brotherhood. Fear God. Honor the king."
> *—1 Peter 2:17 NKJV*

10. In the story that Jesus told of the Good Samaritan, who would you say the priest and Levite represent? (Who would we compare them to today?) What can you learn from their example?

_____

_____

_____

_____

_____

11. John mentions a man named Bill Wilson and how he reaches out to over 20,000 impoverished children in New York City and cities across the country through *Metro Ministries*.

a. Is there an outreach at your church or in your community like *Metro Ministries*? What are a few ways that we can help ministries like this in order to honor the poor?

_____

_____

_____

_____

b. **Read** James 1:27. How does this Scripture define true, pure religion?

_____

_____

_____

_____

> ### LESSONS *from* LEADERS
> "Preach the Gospel every day; if necessary, use words."
> –*St. Francis of Assisi*[5]

12. God doesn't just want us to honor the poor—He wants us to honor people on *all* levels. There are people who are hurting in every economic, educational and ethnic background known to man who desperately need to experience the genuine love of Christ.

a. **Write out** and **take to heart** 2 Corinthians 5:20, describing the mission each of us has as a believer.

_____

_____

_____

_____

b. Meditate on this *personalized* message of Isaiah 50:4 AMP. Speak it out loud over your life daily until it becomes deeply rooted in your spirit.

> "The Lord God has given me the tongue of a disciple and of one who is taught that I should know how to speak a word in season to him who is weary. He wakens me morning by morning; He wakens my ear to hear as a disciple [as one who is taught]."

INSTANT Replay

"When you honor people, you will not ignore or speak rudely to those God brings across your path; rather you walk in a divine flow that brings the living waters of heaven to the thirsty in heart."
—John Bevere (Page 204)

DIG Deeper

You are GOD'S LINK to the unsaved people around you. The question is, are you a *missing link* or a bridge over which God's love can readily cross to touch the hearts of those who are hurting?

Second Corinthians 5:20 declares that we are God's *ambassadors*. An *ambassador* is "a *minister* of the highest rank employed by a prince or state to manage the public concerns of his own prince or state, **representing** the power and dignity of his sovereign [superior]."[6] In other words, we represent God to everyone with whom we come in contact; Jesus Christ, the Prince of Peace, has called, or employed, us to demonstrate His power and dignity and manage His public concerns.

Are you ready to be a full-time ambassador for God, honoring people everywhere you go? Then get ready to live life on a whole new level of adventure! Take a few minutes to think about the places you'll visit and

Ponder the Principle

"...Now wherever we go [God] uses us to tell others about the Lord and to spread the Good News like a sweet perfume (NLT). For we are to God the *fragrance of Christ* among those who are being saved and among those who are perishing" (NKJV).

—2 Corinthians 2:14,15
[Word in brackets added for clarification and emphasis.]

the people you'll meet during the next week. In each situation, you'll have the opportunity to be a sweet smelling fragrance of Christ. Here are some practical ways to show honor to others:

BE A RADIANT REPRESENTATION OF GOD'S GOODNESS!
- Smile
- Look people in the eyes when they speak
- Offer a kind "Hello" or "Good Morning"
- Compliment them for something they did
- Give a small gift when it isn't necessary
- Thank people for helping you
- Hold the door open for others
- Call or address people by name
- Help someone with a task
- Let people know they are important

Add to the list your own God-inspired ideas and have fun being a blessing to others!

_____

_____

_____

_____

INSTANT Replay

"What's most important is that you ask God to put true honor in your heart for all people. If you try to honor without it residing in your heart, it will come out fake, or at best, shallow. It will actually have the opposite effect of what you hope."
—John Bevere (Page 208)

Pray and ask God to put *true honor* in your heart for all people; ask Him to lead you by His Spirit and empower you to impact the lives of those you meet for eternity. As you honor others in practical ways, becoming a radiant representation of God's goodness, opportunities to share the Gospel will open up to you like never before.

At the end of the day, or as you get ready in the morning, take 5 or 10 minutes to *journal your journey*—jot down the

LESSONS from LEADERS

"People don't care how much you know, until they know how much you care."

—*John Maxwell*[7]

highlights of what took place. Who were you able to encourage or help? What was their response? Were you able to tell them about Jesus in any way? How did it make you feel inside?

Journal *Your* Journey
Date Started: _____

_____

_____

_____

_____

_____

_____

_____

_____

_____

_____

_____

_____

Date Completed: _____

Hide in Your Heart

HONOR PRINCIPLE 12
Honor is due, first and foremost, unto God. Out of a heart of honor for God, honor for all others will flow. As we maintain a heart of humility and a reverential fear of the Lord, we will be able to freely give and receive honor.

AT THE HEART OF IT ALL

"Humility and *the fear of the Lord* bring wealth and honor and life."
—Proverbs 22:4 NIV

Throughout this study on honor, we have focused our attention on *giv-ing* honor to others. But how can we obtain honor? What must we do to be valued, esteemed highly and respected by others? Surprisingly, the key to giving honor and getting honor is one and the same—hav-ing a heart of *humility*.

Proverbs 22:4 puts it plainly: Humility and the fear of the Lord bring honor. The two go hand in hand, but humility is the foundation. Without humility, we cannot have a reverential fear of the Lord because a spirit of pride keeps us from seeing our desperate need for God. Pride places *self* on the throne of our hearts, and everything revolves around us. It was pride found in the heart of Lucifer that caused him to *dishonor* God and seek to be worshiped. And it was pride that perma-nently separated him and a portion of the angels from the Father.

HUMILITY

Freedom from pride and arrogance; humbleness of mind; a modest estimation of one's self worth; a deep sense of unworthiness in the sight of God...submission to the divine will.

– American Dictionary of the English Language, **Noah Webster 1828**

Andrew Murray was a minister for over 60 years and author of more than 200 books. His life's theme was the "casting of self" upon Christ.[8] Read this insightful excerpt from his book *Humility.*

> "**Humility,** *the place of entire dependence on God,* is, from the very nature of things, the first duty and highest virtue of man. It is the root of every virtue. And so **pride,** or *the loss of this humility,* is the root of every sin and evil. It was when the now fallen angels began to look upon themselves with self-satisfaction that they were led to disobedience and were cast down from the light of heaven into outer darkness.

Ponder these Principles

"...I warn everyone among you not to estimate and think of himself more highly than he ought [not to have an exaggerated opinion of his own importance], but to rate his ability with sober judgment, each according to the degree of faith apportioned by God to him."
–Romans 12:3 AMP

"...A man can receive nothing [he can claim nothing, he can take unto himself nothing] except as it has been granted to him from heaven. [A man must be content to receive the gift which is given him from heaven; there is no other source.]"
–John 3:27 AMP

"Pride lands you flat on your face; humility prepares you for honors."
–Proverbs 29:23 The Message

When the serpent breathed the poison of his pride—*the desire to be like God—*into the hearts of our first parents, they, too, fell from their high estate [*place of honor*] into all the wretchedness in which man is now sunk. In all heaven and earth, pride and self-exaltation are the gate and the curse of hell."[9]
[Words bolded, italicized and added in brackets for emphasis.]

The more that pride is rooted in our soul, the more difficult it will be for us to give and receive honor. Honoring others—esteeming them and placing high value on them—is, in and of itself, an act of humility. It takes our attention off of self and puts it on others.

So where does humility come from? Is it something we develop on our own? Murray continues:

> "...Jesus came to bring humility back to earth, to make us partakers of it, and by it to save us. ...Jesus Christ took the

place and fulfilled the destiny of man by His life of perfect humility. His humility is our salvation. His salvation is our humility.[10]

...Humility is not a thing that will come on its own. It must be made the object of special desire, prayer, faith, and practice. ...It is simply *the sense of entire nothingness, which comes when we see how truly God is all, and in which we make way for God to be all.*[11]

...True humility comes when, in the light of God, we have seen ourselves to be nothing, have consented to part with and cast away self—to let God be all. ...The humble man looks upon every child of God—even the feeblest and unworthiest—and honors him and prefers him in honor as the son of a King."[12]

True honor for all men flows freely from a heart that is humble. Reread the excerpts from Andrew Murray and, in your own words, write out the meaning of *humility* and explain where it comes from.

_____

_____

_____

_____

_____

_____

_____

INSTANT Replay

"To *retain honor*, we must stay *humble* in spirit. No matter how
abundantly God blesses us, we must always remember,
there is nothing we have we weren't given."
—John Bevere (Page 221)

Proverbs 4:5-8 instructs us to get wisdom and get understanding and they will bring us honor. **Write out** and **take to heart** Proverbs 9:10, which defines the starting place for wisdom.

Also **Check out** Proverbs 1:7 and Psalm 111:10

_____

_____

_____

_____

John shared that when we fear the Lord, we will believe and obey God's Word in all areas of our lives—it will be a growing desire. When you read the Word, do you try to make the scriptures fit into your lifestyle? What is the danger of *reading what you believe* instead of *believing what you read*?

_____

_____

_____

_____

_____

_____

Many people, especially new Christians, will often ask, "What does the Lord require of me? What does He want me to do?" **Take to heart** Micah 6:8 for a clear-cut answer to this question.

_____

_____

_____

_____

_____

Check out Proverbs 13:18; 15:5,32   Being quick to repent, having a believing heart and being willing to accept correction are three things that we must have operating in our lives. In your own opinion, how important is accepting correction?

_____

_____

_____

_____

_____

_____

INSTANT Replay

"We will maintain, as well as grow in, honor if we live in the fear of the Lord and walk in true humility. Never forget how great a death Jesus delivered you from. Also remember His love and the value of every individual you come in contact with is just as great. So honor them, as He honored them by giving His life, and you will gain honor, receive rewards, and retain what you've received."
—John Bevere (Page 223)

Prayer for Humility

Father, forgive me for not honoring You and placing value on the people whom You have placed in my pathway. Please grant me the ability to see people as You see them. May my soul be saturated with the sweetness of Your love, and every day, in a practical way, may I show everyone I meet that life with You is sweet. May they taste and see that You, oh Lord, are good (Psalm 34:8).

Lord, develop within me a heart of humility. Let me never forget all that You have forgiven me of and all that You have saved me from. May a reverential fear of You direct my decisions and grant me a heart of honor for You and others.

Thank You for this study, Lord. May it forever become a part of who I am. In Jesus' name, Amen!

EXPRESS YOUR EXPERIENCE

As you finish this final chapter, sit quietly before the Lord. What is He speaking to your spirit? What things stand out to you the most from the entire study? What is the overall impact this teaching has in your life?

---

(1) Quotes on *Keys to Christian Living* (www.tentmaker.org/Quotes/keys.htm, retrieved 8/16/07). (2) *The New Unger's Bible Dictionary*, Merrill F. Unger, R.K. Harrison, Editor (Chicago, IL: Moody Press, 1988) p. 585. (3) *Vine's Complete Expository Dictionary of Old and New Testament Words*, W. E. Vine (Nashville, TN: Thomas Nelson, Inc. 1996) p. 310. (4) Quotes on *Obedience* (www.dailychristianquote.com, retrieved 9/22/07). (5) Quotes on *Witnessing, Missions and Evangelism*, retrieved 7/24/07, see note 4. (6) *American Dictionary of the English Language*, Noah Webster 1828 (San Francisco, CA: Foundation for American Christian Education, 2000). (7) John Maxwell, *Developing the Leader Within You* (Nashville, TN: Thomas Nelson, Inc. 1993) p. 118. (8) *131 Christians Everyone Should Know*, Andrew Murray (www.christianitytoday.com/history/special/131christians/murray.html, retrieved 9/22/07). (9) Andrew Murray, *Humility* (Whitaker House: New Kensington, PA, 1982) pp. 10,11. (10) See note 9, p. 11. (11) See note 9, pp. 13, 12. (12) See note 9, p. 46.

Notes

Notes

Notes

Notes

Notes

THE BAIT OF SATAN
CURRICULUM

Jesus said, "It's impossible that no offenses will come."
–Luke 17:1

A most crucial message for believers in this hour.

"This message is possibly the most important confrontation with truth you'll encounter in your lifetime. The issue of offense – the very core of *The Bait of Satan* – is often the most difficult obstacle an individual must face and overcome."

– John Bevere

INCLUDES:
- 12 30-MINUTE VIDEO SESSIONS ON 4 DVDs
- 12 30-MINUTE AUDIO SESSIONS ON 6 CDs
- BEST-SELLING BOOK THE BAIT OF SATAN
- DEVOTIONAL WORKBOOK
- PROMOTIONAL MATERIALS

A HEART ABLAZE
CURRICULUM

Jesus has never accepted lukewarmness. Rather, He calls for passion! This message will challenge you to exchange a mediocre relationship with God for a vibrant, fiery one.

INCLUDES:
- 12 30-MINUTE VIDEO SESSIONS ON ON 4 DVDs
- 12 30-MINUTE AUDIO SESSIONS ON 6 CDs
- A HEART ABLAZE BEST-SELLING BOOK
- WORKBOOK
- PROMOTIONAL MATERIALS

UNDER COVER
CURRICULUM

Under the shadow of the Almighty, there is liberty, provision and protection. Unfortunately, many don't understand how to find this secret place. In this curriculum you will learn how biblical submission differs from obedience. You will also learn the distinction between direct and delegated authority and how to respond to and overcome unfair treatment.

INCLUDES:
- 12 30-MINUTE VIDEO LESSONS ON 4 DVDs
- 12 30-MINUTE AUDIO LESSONS ON 6 CDs
- BEST-SELLING BOOK UNDER COVER
- DEVOTIONAL WORKBOOK
- PROMOTIONAL MATERIALS

DRAWING NEAR
CURRICULUM

Drawing extensively from his own journey, John has specially written and prepared this *Drawing Near* message to lead you into times of private and intimate communion with God Himself. This devotional kit acts as a treasure map, guiding you around potential pitfalls and breaking through personal barriers leading you into new and glorious realms of a lifelong adventure with God!

INCLUDES:
- 12 30-MINUTE VIDEO SESSIONS ON 4 DVDs
- BEST-SELLING HARDCOVER BOOK DRAWING NEAR
- A PERSONAL DEVOTIONAL JOURNEY TO HIS HEART JOURNAL

BOOKS BY JOHN

The Bait of Satan
Breaking Intimidation
Drawing Near
Driven by Eternity
Enemy Access Denied
Extraordinary
The Fear of the Lord
A Heart Ablaze

Honor's Reward
How to Respond When You Feel Mistreated
Rescued
Thus Saith the Lord
Under Cover
Victory in the Wilderness
The Voice of One Crying

life-transforming truth.
Messenger International.

Messenger International, founded by John and Lisa Bevere, imparts the fear
of the Lord while inspiring freedom through the spoken and written
Word to release people into their fulfilled lives in Christ.

UNITED STATES
P.O. Box 888
Palmer Lake, CO
80133-0888
800-648-1477 (US & Canada)
Tel: 719-487-3000
mail@MessengerInternational.org

AUSTRALIA
Rouse Hill Town Centre
P.O. Box 6444
Rouse Hill NSW 2155
In AUS: 1-300-650-577
Tel: +61 2 9679 4900
aus@MessengerInternational.org

EUROPE
P.O. Box 1066
Hemel, Hempstead HP2 7GQ
United Kingdom
In UK: 0800 9808 933
Tel: +44 1442 288 531
europe@MessengerInternational.org

The Messenger television program broadcasts in over 200 countries
including the U.S. on GOD TV, the Australian Christian
Channel and the New Life Channel in Russia.
Please check your local listings for day and time.

www.MessengerInternational.org

RESCUED

2 hours on 2 CDs **AUDIO THEATER**

Starring:
Roma Downey from *Touched by an Angel*
John Rhys-Davies from *The Lord of the Rings*
Marisol Nichols from the hit TV show *24*

A trapped father. A desperate son. A clock ticking down toward certain death and a fate even more horrible still…

For Alan Rockaway, his teenaged son Jeff, and his new bride Jenny, it's been little more than a leisurely end to a weeklong cruise…

a horrifying crash and even more, a plunge toward the unknown…Everything Alan has assumed about himself is flipped upside down. In the ultimate rescue operation, life or death is just the beginning!

AFFABEL
WINDOW OF ETERNITY

2.5 hours on 4 CDs

FEATURING JOHN RHYS-DAVIES AND A CAST OF HOLLYWOOD ACTORS

AN EPIC AUDIO THEATER PORTRAYING THE REALITY OF THE JUDGMENT SEAT OF CHRIST. GET READY TO BE CHANGED FOREVER…AND PREPARE FOR ETERNITY!

This audio dramatization, taken from John Bevere's book, *Driven by Eternity*, will capture your heart and soul as you experience life on "the other side" where eternity is brought into the present and all must stand before the Great King and Judge. Be prepared for a roller coaster ride of joy, sorrow, astonishment, and revelation as lifelong rewards are bestowed on some while others are bound hand and foot and cast into outer darkness by the Royal Guard!